BAD WORSE WC
The Story of Derby County's Record I

Written comments to the author regarding Bad Worse ...

"I stumbled across this book while on Amazon (as you do) and I'd just like to say what an excellent read it was."

"Just returned from my Easter trip to England, bringing your book with me. Spent this morning reading it through, and must say I liked it very much. Sad isn't it? Enjoying reading about last season :-(. Anyway: Thanks for the good work. Hopefully there will be another one after this season?"

"I have just finished reading 'Bad, Worse, Worst' which I received as a Christmas present from my son and I thought it was excellent, I couldn't put it down once I started reading it. By the way, have they added Kit-Kats to the picture boards outside Pride Park of banned articles that you can't take into the ground yet?"

"A cracking read, I was laughing out loud at my desk"

"Got the book as a Christmas present. Thoroughly enjoying it, a great read. Thanks and more power to your elbow."

"I mean this in the best possible way, but it's cracking toilet reading!"

"Just got a copy of the book for my birthday - already I'm laughing (through the tears). Excellent work."

"...funny as ****!"

"I didn't see my husband for two days whilst he was reading it!"

Also available from Pure Phase Publishing

Who's Pereplotkins? And other Tales from Derby County's 2008/9 Season
By Edgar Smith

First Published in 2008 by Pure Phase Publishing
88 Manor Road, Derby, DE72 3LN

New Edition published 2010

This book has been published independently and is in no way affiliated with
Derby County Football Club

Any comments, enquiries, or feedback should be sent to
s_spaceram@post.com

ISBN: 978-0-9561144-2-6

BAD

WORSE

WORST

The Story of Derby County's Record Breaking 2007/8 Season

By Edgar Smith

PURE PHASE PUBLISHING

Bad Worse Worst New Edition

Bad Worse Worst was first published in November 2008, less than six months after the close of the now infamous 2007/8 season. Some Rams fans had no interest in the book and did not want to be reminded of our record breaking spell in the Premier League. Others read the book and found they quite enjoyed it.

After two years of steady sales, the book has now been reissued as part of the People's History of Football Series. Bad Worse Worst is the first in the series.

The book has a new cover but although several pages longer than the original, the content remains the same. The extra thickness is due entirely to changes in formatting intended make the text easier on the eye.

Introduction

Fewest wins in a season; fewest home wins in a season; fewest away wins in a season; most losses in a season; most away losses in a season; fewest points in a season; fewest goals scored in a season; worst goal difference in a season; fewest goals scored away in a season; first team to be relegated in March; longest winless sequence; failure to score in the most games. Just a few of the Premier League records equaled or broken by Derby County during the 2007/8 season. I'm sure the list isn't completely exhaustive and I wouldn't want to start on all the club records broken. Basically, if being spectacularly bad was a prerequisite, the Derby County side of 2007/8 were on the podium.

Being a Rams supporter wasn't easy. We were either the butt of every football joke going, or even worse, treated with contempt by those who thought our very presence was devaluing the Premier League. One major bookmaker even started paying out on our relegation when the season was barely out of August.

Some, including myself, remained optimistic for as long as possible. For me, the moment of realisation was at one of the Christmas fixtures - I bought a Golden Goal ticket but when I scratched off the time of next goal it read "February".

During the season I maintained a journal. It was never the intention to record the facts that you could read in the newspaper or give my own match reports. What I have tried to do is capture the experience of supporting the Rams, being a football fan and going to matches - as thousands of us do. What I wasn't expecting was for the season to be of record breaking proportions.

The journals originally appeared unedited on Derby County e-zine Ramspace, so thanks to all the readers who kept me motivated to keep writing even when the season was a lost cause (see Appendix - What are The Journals of Derventio?). The journals also contain references to various people: Ramspace editor and my brother Chris; Bob, the Jackal and Simon - all friends who shared the agony, as well as the odd pre and post match pint (see Appendix - Who's Who?).

It's a horror story but don't look away - turn the page and enjoy.

Preface

In May 2006, Derby County returned to local ownership when a consortium lead by local businessman and former Rams vice-chairman Peter Gadsby took control. The previous regime had taken over when the club were on the verge of financial meltdown, for a nominal £3 - one pound each for the three man consortium. Unfortunately, the club was also in financial meltdown on their departure. After reaching the Play-Offs in 2005, the team had only just survived relegation in 2006. The picture was not good on or off the field.

Gadsby and co. stabilised the finances and over the summer recruited Billy Davies to be the Rams new manager. Davies had a superb track record with Championship rivals Preston having reached the Play-Offs in consecutive seasons with very little expenditure and a team devoid of superstars. The Rams were not awash with cash but did have a modest budget for Davies to wheel and deal with. Davies announced that he had a three year plan and a top ten finish was his target for the forthcoming season.

Against the odds, Derby County were promoted in 2007. Literally against the odds - bookies were offering 66/1 against the Rams winning the title and many fans, including myself, made a tidy profit on an each way bet.

Despite such a seemingly amazing achievement, there were mixed views about Davies amongst Rams fans. Firstly, he never stopped reminding us just how amazing his achievements were. Another criticism was the quality of football. The Rams won an impressive 25 games during the season but 19 of these were generally dour single goal victories. Maybe a harsh criticism if viewed through the eyes of a neutral but having sat through many of them, I can say that the critics had a point. Finally, his January 2007 signings were definitely questionable. Derby topped the division in January 2007 but after bringing in seven new players in the transfer window, the Rams went backwards and limped over the finishing line via the Play-Offs. Davies used the post match interview to air a few of his own gripes, the main one being about the lack of an assistant manager (David "Ned" Kelly had been Davies' assistant at Preston but they had enforced Kelly take a years "gardening leave" rather than let him follow Davies to The Rams. Kelly finally joined Davies in the summer of 2007). As usual, Davies reiterated the greatness of his achievement and reminded us yet again that he was way ahead of schedule.

Never mind, we were back in the Premier League after an absence of five years.

This was the third Rams promotion to the top flight I had experienced in my 24 years of spectatorship and it didn't seem too different. On both previous occasions, the first season back had been a struggle and survival had been the target. On both occasions the club had survived before going on to establish themselves for a few years.

Davies' pre season signings didn't exactly set the pulse racing. Andy Griffin was signed, beating off competition from Stoke; Andy Todd, preferring us over West Brom; and we pipped Charlton for our new record singing Robert Earnshaw. Earnshaw had a good track record in the Premier League though, so he was a fair bet to score a dozen goals and keep us up. Davies also recruited heavily for his back room team with several additions to the coaching staff, a DVD analyst and ex-Scotland manager Craig Brown in the vague role of "Football Consultant".

One thing that wasn't in doubt was the commitment of the fans. A record number of season tickets were sold - in fact all available season tickets were sold. For the first time ever the Rams had a waiting list for season tickets. Some cynics, such as myself, wondered how many of the new season ticket holders were more interested in watching the away team but there was no denying the sense of anticipation was high across the city.

When the Rams finally took to the field on August 11th 2007 against Portsmouth, only three of the Rams starting line up had never sampled the Premier League before (including Stephen Pearson who had played in the Scottish equivalent, Champions League and was a current international). The one area where the Premier League experience was really lacking was not on the pitch - as frequently cited - but in the dug out. Was Billy ready for the step up?

Prologue

The Journals of Derventio – Play-Off Final day

May 29th

The story of Wembley:

We set off from Derby at about half eight in the morning, after half an hour of "Is it too *early* yet?", "Is it *too* early yet?", "*Is* it too early yet?", the first bottles were cracked open somewhere between Loughborough and Leicester.

By the time we reached Toddington Services, we were ready for a stop. The number of Derby fans at the services was unbelievable with the queue for the gents almost filling the atrium. We thought we might as well go somewhere discreet outside and I was pointed to a good spot between some skips. When I glanced up mid-flow, I was being overlooked by one of many Roadriders - so much for privacy. I half expected someone to be waiting with some hand-soap and a splash of Brut when I emerged from the other side.

We reached Wembley, no problem, and had already decided that we'd get in an eatery. The original plan of "a pickle tray and 8 pints please" was abandoned as we were genuinely hungry and ready for the "Gurka Valley's" finest by half eleven. This seemed an especially good call as queues for the pub next door snaked down the road and even had stewards (and it was raining). The food was good and even though the Gurkha curry wasn't as good as the pre-QPR one (are Gurkhas out of season?), you couldn't put a price on having waiter service rather than a scrum for a warm pint in a plastic pot.

As I mentioned in previous Journals, two of us were in the Club Wembley seating. There were escalators rather than stairs and the whole scene resembled an airport lounge. After the earlier meal, I never did discover what the "hospitality" entitlement was, although that was as much to do with the number of people queuing as anything else (bearing in mind the section was about a third full, a busy game could be trouble).

There's been a lot of complaints about the empty Club Wembley seats not being redistributed but to be fair most of the 7,000 scattered around were either Derby or West Brom fans (apart from someone behind me who asked "are you supporting Derby or West Ham?" oops!). Splitting the remaining 10,000 would definitely have caused segregation problems. You need a lot of tolerance if trouble is to be avoided. We had to bite our tongue whilst West Brom fans behind us draped flags on neutrals and muttered "Dirty Rams" every time we made a tackle. On the other hand, they had to watch me and the Jackal having a lengthy man-tangle a yard away when Pearo scored (and at the final whistle of course). By the time the Fratellis came on the West Brom fans were gone.

Everyone was in a buoyant mood for the journey home - all until Billy Davies came on the radio. He moaned about the David Kelly situation, sniped at the fans for being impatient with players and generally put the mockers on things. We slammed The View album on and cracked open our remaining supplies.

As my domestic situation had changed dramatically in the past couple of weeks (a new born baby), it was back home for me but within half an hour I'd received a text from my brother saying "Me and Boab in a man tangle to Chelsea Dagger already" (you can guess what the phrase of the day was). What better way to celebrate?

August 2007

11.08.07 Derby County 2-2 Portsmouth

15.08.07 Manchester City 1-0 Derby County

18.08.07 Spurs 4-0 Derby County

25.08.07. Derby County 1-2 Birmingham City

On paper, there was no reason why The Rams shouldn't make a reasonable start to the season. The most difficult game was Spurs away and they are hardly Man Utd are they?

The season couldn't have got off to a better start when Matt Oakley put the Rams ahead after only five minutes and chants of "we are top of the league" could even be heard (even though Sunderland had already beaten Spurs in the lunchtime kick-off). The match finished 2-2 after a very late equaliser by new signing Andy Todd. We all left the ground full of optimism: Derby had more than matched Portsmouth and the new players all looked promising, especially Andy Todd in a midfield role. Even better, the two who hadn't played at the top level before, Fagan and Howard, both looked comfortable with Howard giving Sol Campbell a torrid afternoon. The only nagging concern was the ease with which Portsmouth had scored. We would definitely have to sharpen up at the back now that the quality of finishing had gone up a notch.

The Rams continued to add to the squad with young American midfielder Benny Feilhaber signing for £1m from Hamburg, where he had failed to break into the first team. Feilhaber was billed as a player who would blossom at both club and international level and Davies was keen to tell us what a bargain he had got. A second signing, Finn Mika Vayrynen, was also agreed with PSV Eindhoven but the deal fell through as the Finn picked up a knock when due for his medical.

Next was Man City away. The Rams lost 0-1 but we again gave a fair account of ourselves. An introduction to many elements of the Premier League came in our next fixture against Spurs away. Spurs had suffered two defeats in their first two matches and unbelievably, the press were heaping the pressure on Spurs manager Martin Jol. The third game of the season had become a "must-win" game for Jol and who better to have a "must-win" game against? A hyped up Spurs team took to the field and Derby simply crumbled. The Rams were 3-0 down after only fourteen minutes. In terms of confidence, you could argue that the whole season could be traced back to this match. From this moment on, home sides generally saw the Rams as fair game and in return, the Rams players were often the proverbial "rabbits in the headlights" away from home.

The defeat not only left the players shattered but optimism also began to drain from the fans. In the week following the Spurs match, the Derby Telegraph website revealed that the Rams had completed the signing of an "international midfielder". I, like many others, eagerly clicked on the link to see who would be the man to revive our season. It turned out to be 33 year old League One winger, Eddie Lewis, an American international. With all due respect to Lewis, who is undoubtedly a committed and hard working player, the chances of him reviving Derby's season were extremely slim. Davies has a great way of building up his new signings and said that all his searches for a quality left sided player were coming back to Eddie Lewis. Fans, including myself, couldn't help wondering what kind of scouting systems the club had in place for that to happen.

The following fixture was at home to Birmingham, who had been promoted with us last season. In keeping with the hyperbole of the Premier League, our pre-match conversations contained phrases such as "must-win" and "six pointer". Birmingham, like ourselves, were expected to be in the relegation mix come May and we didn't want to lose ground on them just yet. We also had some tough fixtures on the horizon and having only gained one point so far, this was by far our best opportunity to get on the scoreboard.

The match was a huge let down. 0-1 down within a minute, the Rams were outplayed and lucky to lose only 1-2. For saying there was very little between the two sides last season, there was now a chasm.

The Rams final act of a disappointing August was the deadline day signing of Scottish International striker Kenny Miller from Celtic for around £2.2m. It was clear that we needed more firepower as record signing Robert Earnshaw had already been dropped after a goalless start to the season.

The Journals of Derventio - August

August 1st

The unavoidable question at the moment is - can the Rams survive in the Premiership next season? According to fans of 17 of the 20 Premiership clubs the answer appears to be "no" (survey in the Observer. The other three clubs were: Fulham; Chelsea - who nominated Fulham, Wigan plus A N Other; and us).

I don't envy Billy at all though with the transfer market the way it is. The examples are too numerous to mention but the fees paid for Chopra, Koumas and Kamara, all players who have bombed in the Premiership in the last couple of years are prime examples. An outsider looking at the fees paid for West Brom players (with Curtis Davies due to leave for around £8 million) might assume that the Baggies are a footballing Harlem Globetrotters, not Championship also-rans. Let's face it - if they couldn't cause our defence any problems (with due respect - a good Championship defence but no more) then I can't see Carvalho or Vidic going off with stress before facing Fulham or Wigan.

So where does that leave us? Sunderland are well on course to spend £20-30m if they close the deals they're currently involved in but are only getting crumbs from the Premiership table and don't look much better off to me. I, for one, am pleased that we haven't followed this approach. Birmingham have spent less but after the recent farcical episode with Hossam Ghaly** and botched attempt to sign Mido, you have to wonder to what degree Bruce's signings are driven by desperation (from what I could gather, Ghaly turned up for training, thought "this lot are bobbins", or the Egyptian equivalent; Brum thought "this guy's an idiot" and the whole deal was off. Surely unprecedented?). So far we've avoided both inflated fees and desperation but for how long? Billy has promised that the squad would soon become unrecognisable so we should be in for an interesting couple of weeks.

West Brom sold Kamara for £6m, Koumas for £5m, Paul McShane for £2.5m and Nathan Ellington for £3.5m

**Hossam Ghaly was to join the Rams on loan during the January transfer window.*

August 3rd

I've still not been accepted by Craig "single, straight, here for dating, serious relationships" Fagan as a friend on myspace whilst several others have. What have Melissa from Texas, BustyBrooke from Zimbabwe and Exotic Gangsta Barbie from Virginia got that I haven't?

There are some football fans though. His latest message reads: "alright fagan you should get back to city* you was fuckin ace.every game you always took the piss out of everyone you ran at with the ball. your a great player".

I can only think he read our site and didn't like it?

Hull City. Ironically, Fagan was to return there later in the season.

August 5th

A few weeks ago I wondered why on earth Neil Lennon would leave Champions League regulars Celtic, allegedly spurn the Premiership and sign for a lower league East Midlands team *(Nottingham Forest).* The rumour, according to Ted McMinn on Radio Derby, is "tens of thousands of pounds a week". Ted triumphantly added that judging by Lennon's performance, his "legs had gone" already (an opinion shared by others at the match).

(Ted was spot on. Lennon was released by Forest in January and allowed to join Wycombe Wanderers on a free transfer)

Talking of money, it occurred to me that we have reached a point in history (that sounds a bit dramatic doesn't it?) when the cost of a match ticket for most games is the same or less than that of a replica shirt. That's not a dig at The Rams as I'm sure it's the same all over (fans of London clubs are probably thinking "blimey gav'nor, I can get the whole kit and a track suit"...or more likely..."I say Jeremy these northern oiks etc.") anyway, thinking back to my youth, a shirt would be about three times the price of a ticket (at least four or five times the price of standing - I won't labour this point though, it will only make me sound old).

August 7th

How about this for damning someone with faint praise in the Derby Telegraph? When summarising Richard Jackson's Rams career, the article alludes to him not being a particularly attacking full-back before adding "[when he did come forward] he showed he could deliver a cross, as we saw in the victory over West Ham United at Upton Park in January 2005." It doesn't flatter Jacko to think that the last time he attacked was two and a half years ago and it still sticks in the memory like the sighting of a rare bird! As rumours circulate that Jonno may be next to leave, the draft copy reads "Johnson was no Franz Beckenbauer but did once successfully pass to the feet of Rams player 15 months ago".

A more recent sighting of Jacko's attacking prowess was his cross for Howard's header at Cardiff last year. It was also one of his last starts. *(Rams full back Richard Jackson was about to join Luton Town on a free transfer)*

August 9th

I was at a meeting a couple of weeks ago when someone offered to show a video-phone clip of the Play-off final (Why? I don't know - but do you need an excuse?). A young chap piped up with "I hate that team with a passion" Yes, he was a Forest fan (he was there to experience "a meeting". Rule no.1 - Have a good idea of other peoples football allegiances before you make a stupid comment like that. Otherwise you may experience unexpected and unexplainable bouts of misfortune during your career e.g. being passed over for promotion in favour of a quiet chap who sits in the corner sipping tea from a Derby County mug). It struck me at the time how little his comment bothered me whereas years ago I would have been fuming.

During the late 80's and 90's, when Forest and Derby were generally in the same division, the rivalry was always intense whilst Forest had a smug and patronising fondness for Notts County (Notts, meanwhile hated Forest with a passion). Fast forward to pre-season 2007 and most Rams fans viewed the Forest team at the Cloughy match with a mixture of amusement and pity, whilst down the A52 the previous night, Forest and Notts County fans fought on the pitch after a "friendly" between the two clubs (the indignity of it!). Have Forest fans' passions re-focused to a more realistic target?

(The same meeting this week was interrupted by the Chair's phone ringing - a Casio Keyboard version of Robbie Williams' Angels. I've decided that particular group is not the best use of my time).

August 12th

(Written after the 2-2 draw against Portsmouth).

Observations from the first week back in the Premiership:

- Derby are still a low priority on Match Of The Day.
- It is often said about Robert Earnshaw that his contribution amounts to whether he scores or not. He didn't.
- It is true to say that mistakes are very costly in the Premiership.
- Any mention of Andy Todd will also mention his dad. (Remembered by Rams fans over 40 as one of our greatest ever players. Remembered by Rams fans under 40 as one of our worst ever managers).

- A portion of onion rings from Frankie and Benny's (£2.75 for about 8) is daylight robbery. I expected the waitress to serve them with a stocking over her head.

- Even the joy of a late equaliser can be spoilt when someone knocks your Prada shades off in the celebration (I was neither aggressor nor victim by the way).

- Many of Derby's players must live high up in the Peak District judging by some of the all terrain vehicles in the car park. Looking at one particular beast Jackal commented "I half expect the Ant Hill Mob to pile out the back of that". The registration was J8NNO.

August 13th

Further observations of the Premiership - the Premiership is above the law when it comes to work permits. At the Home Office it's a case of "Premiership players to the left in the green channel, genocide survivors and Football League wannabes to the right - red channel".

About this time last year the Rams tried to sign experienced USA international Josh Wolff (48 caps) but were denied as he was a few games, literally a few games, short of the required quota. This season we try to sign Benny Feilhaber (8 caps - well below the quota) and there's no problem. Claude Davis was also short but again - no problem. Man City sign two new players and "neither Bulgarian striker Bojinov, 21, or Croatian defender Corluka, 21, met the strict criteria required." according to the BBC but both played on Saturday.

We also have 6 Nigerian international strikers in the Premiership (Kanu, Yakubu, Utaka, Aghahowa, Martins, Anichebe); either Nigeria play the most attacking formation ever or some of these chaps don't play the required 75% of games. Admittedly not all need a permit* but every game played is one from someone else's quota. I daresay there are also other

Nigerian strikers elsewhere in Europe and even Nigeria itself competing for the same places.

I've often thought the whole system discriminates against the lower division sides who are barred from signing good value players appropriate to their level. The likes of Portsmouth and Bolton can sign any N'Tom, M'Dick or Harridino to sit on the bench for two years whilst the likes of Accrington, Hereford and Forest are denied signing, for example, a non-international Croat or Ukranian who could play 40 games a season.

*You may remember Yakubu's whirlwind romance and subsequent marriage to a lady of European descent in the weeks between Derby's work permit application for Yakubu being declined and Yakubu signing for Portsmouth with his new European passport. Yakubu went on to score a hatful as Pompey romped to the league title. Derby narrowly avoided relegation before going into receivership. I'm not bitter though.

August 15th

Conversation at work today:

Me: Are you looking forward to Man City tomorrow?

Colleague: Yes. I've got my Amnesty International t-shirt ready.

(Man City chairman and ex-Thailand Prime Minister Thaksin Shinawatra was being investigated for Human Rights violations at this time).

August 16th

Can you remember Mark de Vries? Just to re-cap: rubbish Dutch striker signed by Leicester during Craig Levein's disastrous tenure. He scored 1 goal in 16 matches during his first season and then 3 league goals the following season. He was then farmed out to Dutch clubs for the next year and a half. Missing presumed dead in the eyes of many. Ok, keep this in mind.

Over the summer Leicester City were the subject of huge changes; a new Chairman, new manager, an injection of cash, high expectations and a teams worth of new players, including strikers Carl Cort and DJ Campbell to add to not-too-bad existing strikers Hume, Fryatt and Hammond. So when the new look, souped-up, sexed-up Foxes took to the field for the first game of the season, who should be leading the line but, you've guessed it, yer man de Vries. For those who missed the result, Leicester failed to score and lost 1-0. At home. To Blackpool.

(post-script - according to Martin Allen, de Vries was glorious on Saturday so I may yet be eating my words).

(De Vries was released by Leicester mid season and joined Dundee United. The new look Leicester used three managers before being relegated in May).

August 19th

When Pride Park was built, it was modelled on Middlesbrough's Riverside stadium with a number of minor improvements based on Boro's first year in their new ground. The builders will probably be pleased to know that in a recent survey of Premiership stadiums by the Observer, Pride Park finished one place above the Riverside. Pride Park was 19th and the Riverside 20th. Talking about the Observer, you may have noticed our correspondent featured in The Verdict today. I sorted it out in the week, balancing the chance of appearing in the nations best broadsheet against the fact that our man at the match was "doing a Leo Sayer*" around London. Thankfully, he delivered the goods. The same man also bumped into Chris Riggott on the train home. Riggott apparently expressed his fondness for the Rams before asking some probing questions about our current defenders - someone tell Billy quick!

*Foreign readers - rhyming slang for an "all-dayer". That probably doesn't make sense either - drinking intoxicating liquor for a prolonged period spread across the course of a day.

August 22nd

It seems Dean Sturridge remains undeterred in his ambition to emulate his hero Ian Wright. After failing to break the Arsenal goalscoring record, or indeed sign for them in the first place, Studger has now embarked on a media career as a co-commentator for Radio Derby. I initially thought Studger would be as suited to radio work about as well as he's suited to playing centre-back; to be fair though he sounds alright. On Saturday though, I did notice his subtle change from the familiar "We need to..." to the more detached "Derby County need to..." as Tottenham started to rack the goals up!

(Sturridge only lasted one season with Radio Derby and wouldn't be regarded as the most popular pundit ever.)

August 23rd

With Bolton languishing at the bottom of the league (I'm using "languishing at the bottom of the league" about someone else just in case I don't get chance for a while) and Diouf and Anelka seemingly on the way, I'm sure it won't be long before people are questioning the appointment of Sammy Lee. It wouldn't be the first coach or assistant manager to step up and fail (remember Les Reed anyone?). After an intense summer of study (reading the autobiographies of Niall Quinn, Lars Leese and Stan Ternant by the pool) my mate Simon has the following theory on the matter: the coach is generally the class joker, leading the club farting competitions and the like. Then one day, he puts a suit on and starts asking people to turn up on time - it just doesn't work.

An example he gave was from Lars Leese book (German ex-Barnsley 'keeper during their brief spell in the Premiership). One minute cheeky chappie John Hendrie was arriving late for the team coach, clutching a bag full of McDonald's. The next minute he was manager (he was a player at the time but an internal appointment nonetheless). A graph showing Barnsley's fortunes would show a downward trend for approximately eight years after that episode.

(As predicted, Sammy Lee was sacked as the season progressed…and Bolton didn't).

August 26th

(The following entry relates to Derby's 1-2 home defeat by Birmingham. A match we started with great optimism but ended fearing the worst).

The less said about yesterdays game the better, a classic case of a good day being ruined by 90 minutes in the middle. One minute we were sitting in the sunshine drinking Belgian strawberry beer and having a good laugh then bundling out of a taxi on Pride Park feeling a great sense of *joie de vivre*; moments later I was sitting in the East Stand thinking - "I'm in the same stand, watching the same two teams as this time last year - but this time it's cost me forty quid. Now the Premiership hype has subsided, the emperors new clothes are revealed...and it's a Birmingham City shirt". By the time I'd finished this psychobabble we were 1-0 down.

After my comments about the cars parked outside the ground a couple of weeks ago, there was a few people taking photos of the vehicles on display (not because of my piece, I'm sure I'm a latecomer to the sport of car-spotting). The vehicle of the week was definitely a huge "Hummer" which I suggested was a crime against the environment; the Jackal said it was at least a crime against good taste. I've no idea who the owner is but maybe they could put it to good use and check out some of Iraq's Asia Cup winning squad? Another point of note was the empty "Football Consultant" bay. We could certainly have done with some consultation on Saturday; hopefully Craig* was discovering an undiscovered genius somewhere. I believe Steve Howard also had the honour of joining Simon's self proclaimed "stalkers gallery" on his phone. This includes amongst others - Brian Lara, Dean Saunders and the drummer from the Futureheads.

*Craig Brown - appointed by Billy Davies in a capacity that still remains unknown.

August 27th

In times of adversity, there's sometimes nothing better than having a cheap dig at someone. So here we go: Vincent Pericard - this is your life. Stoke's ex-Juventus striker Vincent Pericard was recently jailed for 4 months after the ex-Juventus man lied about a speeding offence (he claimed his father-in-law was driving. His father-in-law hasn't been in Britain for several years). Did I mention he used to play for Juventus? The Juventus link is a curious one which seems to have served Big Vinny well over the years. His salary was revealed during the trial to be £190,000 a year; not bad for a fella who has never scored double figures in a season nor even a top flight goal.

So what was Pericard's Juventus career all about? After a quick search, I soon discovered it consisted of less than half an hour in a "dead rubber" Champions League match watched by 8,500 in Turin. It is likely that Pericard tried to swap shirts with his own players after the match. Tie-ups, shin pads and jock straps infused with the sweat of Juve players appeared on ebay hours after the match - probably. In short, the sort of career that makes David Jones feel aggrieved that he didn't get a testimonial at Man Utd.

The reason I find this of interest is that a few years ago I read a book about a chap who followed Liechtenstein, at one point their 'keeper had the chance to sign for Juve but didn't because it was widely believed that Juve sign any old youngster in the knowledge that they can milk the added value of the Juve connection in the transfer market. "Does this really happen?" I wondered. I don't know if this is the case with Pericard but imagine this scenario: he plays 2 games for Saint Etienne and is then signed by Juve (true). After his life changing half an hour the ruse is well under way, all that is needed is someone to sign him. Where would be your first port of call? Pericard signs for Harry Redknapp's Portsmouth shortly after. Co-incidence or not, you can guarantee that his career earnings to date out strip his pie-munching, more effective colleague at Stoke - Jon Parkin, who carries the less glamorous pre-fix of "ex-Macclesfield".

(Pericard failed to regain his place in the Stoke line-up before being loaned out to Southampton for the seasons run-in. He failed to score for the Saints in five appearances).

August 27th

Text received today:

"Uncle seen giles* at eastwood v ilson town this afternoon. Drives a porsche 4x4. We'll soon know who drives that hummer with this process of elimination in force". This came after an earlier text regarding a sighting of Pearo in a 3 litre Audi.

Onto other news, I see Yakubu has had his work permit application turned down on the eve of his move to Everton. Evidently his marriage didn't work out (see August 13th for full work permit moan).

*Giles Barnes

August 28th

Email received today:

"The Hummer belongs to Robert Earnshaw. Saw him struggling to dismount the beast before the Portsmouth game (I doubt stepladders are included in the price.)"

I'm glad I solved this one before I'd gone through the whole team, got a restraining order and had all the inconvenience of that.

Aside from driving a Monster Truck, another way of looking macho would be to go on Match of The Day and Sky Sports, rough up some defenders and score loads of goals. A somersault afterwards would be a nice touch as well.

August 30th

Music news from the Jackal:

"Went to the reserves last night...I'd say about a 1000 people there....Steve Bloomer's watching followed by de de de de Stevie Howard at 1000 decibels before the game, at half time, when they came out for the 2 half, and at the end of the game."

September 2007

Premier League Table 1st September 2007

		P	W	D	L	Pts	GD
17	Spurs	4	1	0	3	3	0
18	Bolton	4	1	0	3	3	-2
19	Fulham	4	1	0	3	3	-2
20	Derby	4	0	1	3	1	-6

Results:

01.09.07 Liverpool 6-0 Derby County

17.09.07 Derby County 1-0 Newcastle

22.09.07 Arsenal 5-0 Derby County

29.09.07. Derby County 1-1 Bolton Wanderers

September got off to the worst possible start with the Rams suffering a 6-0 hammering at Anfield on the first day of the month. In the midweek prior to the game, Derby had been knocked out of the Carling cup by Championship side Blackpool. Like many clubs, the Rams had used the squad and given a run out to a few fringe players including Bob Malcolm, a midfielder who had not featured since February, and Mo Camara, a full back played on the wing, who had not played since January. Inexplicably, Davies started both players at Anfield (needless to say, neither player finished the game with both substituted by 63 minutes).

There is no shame in losing at Anfield, even getting hammered at Anfield but it was yet another signpost to Derby's eventual plight. The Match of The Day pundits had sniggered at the Rams defending and bookies Paddy Power announced that they would now pay out to anyone who had bet on Derby to be relegated. The match also marked Andy Todd's last appearance for several months. After an awful display, it was announced that he was carrying an unspecified back injury and would not be seen until January. Rumours circulated that a post match discussion with Davies was the actual reason for his thenceforth absence. Whatever the truth was, Todd's stock had fallen a long way since his Houchen-esque equaliser against Pompey, barely three weeks ago.

Due to an international break, the Rams next fixture was over a fortnight away, a televised Monday night match against Newcastle. Kenny Miller made his debut and the unexpected happened - the Rams won 1-0 courtesy of a spectacular Kenny Miller goal. The mood changed dramatically. Not only had we won but we had deserved to win against mid-table Newcastle. There was no doubt that we'd pick up plenty more points across the season. Whether it would be enough to stay up remained to be seen but it was a start at least.

Five days later, our chins were back on the floor. We were again battered away from home, this time 0-5 by Arsenal at the Emirates Stadium. Optimists could still fall back on the argument that most teams lose away to Arsenal, so what? But there was a growing feeling, especially amongst the media, that Derby were out of their depth.

The final Saturday of the month was another "must-win six pointer" against Bolton at home. Bolton's start to the season was nearly as bad as ours and carrying on some of the euphoria of the Newcastle game, we were almost expecting to win. The game ended 1-1. It could have been better, it could have been worse. In a month that contained two heavy, heavy defeats, we had actually gained four points - little did we know that it would represent more than a quarter of our final total.

The Journals of Derventio – September

September 2nd

Another Saturday when I'll avoid dwelling on the game, only to say that losing away to Liverpool, however heavily, isn't going to get you relegated - unless it's last game of the season and you need a win to stay up. A bit of laughter in the dark was provided by the Observer; writing about Robert Malcolm (sic). The report read "...his bald pate went crimson for the mistake that gave Torres a second Premiership goal". I'm sure the forums are alive with debate about team selection and tactics. Personally, I thought Billy missed a trick which could have helped no end - he should have asked Earnshaw to park his Hummer on the goal-line behind Bywater.

Preston have also had a shocking start to the season and Simmo* has attributed it to a most unusual source - Preston's choice of running out music. Now this may sound odd but picture the scene: Preston v. Colchester, probably not a huge crowd; Preston have had an indifferent start and the players need all the backing the crowd can give them. So what comes blaring out the Deepdale PA as the teams take to the field? UB40's reggae-lite version of the Elvis ballad "Wise Men Say". Preston's players shuffle on and Colchester roll them over 3-0. "The song has to go" said Simmo "You need a buzz when the players come running out. We have to get the place rocking".

Ex-Rams winger Paul Simpson

September 3rd

So Paddy Power are paying out on The Rams being relegated already? A cheap publicity stunt if ever there was one. Firstly, how many people would have placed an odds-on single bet that they couldn't collect for 9 months? I would imagine the amount of money involved was significantly less than paid-for advertising space in any of the papers covering the story. If big money was involved, any business would sit on it for 9 months for cash flow or even the interest.

So what if the unexpected happens and The Rams stay up? Will Mr. Patrick Power be weeping into his Guinness? No he'll be rubbing his hands at another round of free publicity…so he will.

September 7th

The Rams bandwagon now seems to have done a definite u-turn. Firstly, we had unknown "Rams fans" coming out of the woodwork (promotion time), then we had a retreat and silence (indifferent start) and now we have a new breed of hitherto unknown football experts coming out the woodwork with "Derby are crap" and the likes. Now hits are up and my anonymity is not as good as it was, I have to be a bit careful; but I'll give you a couple of examples:

First off, someone who said "how sad are you?" (an irritating phrase in any context) after the Jackal started a sentence by saying "we're all big Derby fans". The person who made the comment had tried to obtain play-off tickets, enjoyed an all-dayer on play-off final day and celebrated the promotion harder than most. Enthusiasm followed by derision. A swing usually reserved for a quickly forgotten final of X-Factor.

The second was relatively innocuous but I daresay common; someone admiring my young son saying "don't grow up to support Derby County they're rubbish", a comment unlikely to have been made if we were half way up the Championship and below the mainstream radar.

I did actually unearth a new Rams fan at work who declared himself after the Tottenham debacle. However, when I said "shocking result Saturday wasn't it?" he replied "how did they get on, I didn't catch it?" This was the following Friday. I suppose he doesn't really count.

To quote Chris in the Ramspace Barometer "It's been a shocking start and the squad has hardly been transformed in the manner we were told it would be. However, there's no point moaning about it, the lads need us more than ever so we say keep the faith and let's turn it round." Couldn't have said it better myself.

September 8th
Apparently our football consultant is working for BBC Scotland today. When he was appointed it was said that a key part of his role would be to strengthen our hand in the world transfer market. If this is what he does on international weekend, is it any wonder we've got so many Scots in the squad now? *(At this point McEveley, Teale, Pearson and Miller were all in the Scotland squad, with Steve Howard in the Scotland 'B' team. Ex-Ranger Bob Malcolm was also on the books - more of him later).*

September 9th
It looks like indie fashion has finally reached the mainstream with Ian Wright appearing on Match of the Day wearing cardigan, jeans and desert boots. The daffodils for his back pocket are on order for Wednesday.

September 12th
What a dull couple of weeks it's been with the double whammy of the transfer window closing and an international break. It's got to the point where I can't even be bothered to look on the internet at lunch, whereas only a fortnight ago I couldn't wait. There's only so much I want to know about Gerrard's toe and Healy's calf - which is not a lot in the first place. I spied the Derby Telegraph in someone's bag at work today and thought I'd have a quick look - things are so quiet that the back page headline was about

Emile Heskey. Gerald Mortimer didn't even offer one comment or opinion on The Rams in his weekly page of sport.

I nearly had a story at the weekend but not quite. Whilst queuing up at Sainsburys, I glanced across the checkouts to see David Jones with his trolley full of goodies (meaning I've seen him more than the average Rams fan this season). As we were leaving around the same time, I kept him in the corner of my eye. I approached my car and started to unpack, noticing that parked next to me in the parent and child section was a massive 4x4. Looking over my other shoulder, I saw Mr. Jones ambling towards me (no children or pushchairs in tow). Surely not? I thought. He then stopped and stood. I looked around again - he was still there. If I was the Premiership footballer in this scene I probably would have said to "yeah, yeah, it's me". Then it dawned on him that his car was parked a couple of rows along. So off he went to his perfectly normal car, no 4x4, no illegal parking, no scandal - a non-story in a slow news week.

September 14th

An interesting story on the Derby Telegraph website today: apparently touts are trying to sell tickets for the Newcastle game online for £203. The last time I looked, the club had downgraded the game from "Gold" to "Silver" and knocked nearly a tenner off the price of a ticket. At the time of writing tickets are still available at about thirty quid. I'm no economist but the laws of supply and demand aren't working here.

The Telegraph goes on to write about how despicable a practice this is and that the tickets are being supplied by Rams season ticket holders. The Telegraph then lists all the sites involved complete with hyperlinks. "If you've bought a season ticket and are feeling disappointed, just click here to punt your ticket on for a huge profit"* The Telegraph should get commission.

*The Telegraph didn't print this, legal eagles, it's just what some cynics might think.

On a serious note, I wonder if this is why season tickets sold out so quickly? You could buy a season ticket for about £400. A seat for a sold out game could quite easily be sold for £100+ to any number of people: a Geordie or Mackem as above who missed out on the first 3,000; a Surrey based Man U fan with no legitimate means of getting a ticket; a "one game a season" neutral with a bit of cash wanting to see Chelsea or Arsenal; and the ultimate enemy - those born and living within the city walls whose allegiances lie elsewhere ("I've supported them since I was a kid" they claim; you also used to wet the bed and wear teddy bear romper suits - do you still do that? Well, grow up then). It wouldn't take many games to make a profit.

September 15th

Driving past Pride Park this afternoon I saw a billboard advertising the Newcastle game with a picture of Earnshaw and the strap-line "Earnie your stripes" the pun being the addidas stripes on his shoulder and the Newcastle kit (in case you needed that pointing out!). Surely a better one would have been Private Earnshaw sat atop his Hummer, in combat fatigues, with the same strap-line. Possibly pointing some military hardware at Michael Owen.

September 16th

The Observer coverage of the Hull match reads "[a Jay-Jay Okocka run]...led to David Livermore making it 1-1 from Fagan's flick on".
Did I imagine the last year? Was he on a "try before you buy" deal? Or did this reporter just think he'd been injured for a while?*

This was truly visionary journalism - as earlier mentioned, Fagan was to return to Hull later in the season.

September 19th

(The following entry refers to The Rams first and only victory of the season. A 1-0 win against Newcastle. Unfortunately for me, the Monday night fixture was one of the few home matches during the season that I didn't attend!)

I had every faith in us winning on Monday night, so much so that I told anyone who'd listen at work what a good bet we were (9/2 to win). After chatting to a colleague about it, he convinced me that if I really must bet on the Rams, Derby to be winning at half time would be the best bet. The logic being that if we were to take the lead, it would be from a first-half frenzy and the odds would probably be better anyway. Coming from man who won a couple of hundred quid last week on a line including Dundee and East Fife, I thought I should temper my optimism with some of his pragmatism. I went on-line in the afternoon and after getting bombarded by all the "match specials" I had 4 bets: Draw at Half Time - Derby to win Full-Time; Derby to win 2-0; Derby to score a penalty (why?); Derby winning at Half time - Draw at Full-Time. I won a grand total of £0. Whatever happened to a simple home win?

I ended up watching the game with the Jackal on Setanta; not the best coverage. I offered to "accidentally" destroy one of Rockin' Bob's ornaments if we scored (mutual friend and Jackals landlord) but by the time I could dive headlong into his multi-coloured headless bust mosaic lamp, the goal had been and gone. Sentanta were too busy showing Leacock having a man-tangle with a Newcastle defender. At least the lamp (and therefore my Bolton ticket - a freebie from Bob) remained in tact. (Only joking Bob of course. I wouldn't have risked electrocution and shrapnel injuries at the same time)

September 21st

Quick, someone phone Sky Sports! Someone has been discovered in a remote area of the Peak District who Sky are yet ask about Jose Mourinho's departure.

September 22nd

Text from Bob re: the September 19th entry:

"That multi coloured bust was expensive as well, you'd have needed 1 of the bets to have come in! I enjoyed clearing up countless empties and tops when I got in anyway"

September 23rd

(The following entry follows Derby's 6-0 drubbing by Arsenal at the Emirates Stadium)
In light of recent results, I was absolutely gutted at Saturday tea-time. How did Liverpool not beat Birmingham? I had what I thought was a great value bet (Sheff Wed and Stoke both to win at home, both above evens) and thought I'd chuck Liverpool on the end to win an extra fiver. No value but after our demolition at Anfield I thought Liverpool had stopped dropping points like this.

Simon was in today's Observer sharing his thoughts on the game; anyone who has spoken to him about football for more than two minutes would probably agree that his insights have been worthy of a national stage for years! I hope Stephen Bywater isn't a reader though after Simon labelled him "chocolate wrists" in the paper for his habit of getting two hands on the ball but failing to keep it out the net. Stephen, if you want his address I'm sure I could find it in exchange for a few match tickets and a replica shirt - don't sign it thanks.

Bob was in the Emirates hospitality, his afternoon summarised as "had several scoops before the game...boss had to keep me in check when I was brandishing "virtual yellow card" at Adebayor". I hope he cleared up his empties and bottle tops afterwards.

September 24th

Reports in today's paper (quoting yesterday's paper) claim that investors are trying to buy the Rams for £30 million (the Telegraph says "a figure of £30m for what is currently a Premier League club appears low". I think the use of the word "currently" in this sentence suggests some pessimism at the Telegraph).

A rise in value from £3 to £30m in about three years is some financial turnaround, just how JK* probably imagined it - unfortunately for him, he's not around to get £10m for his solitary golden nugget. Altogether now - "*Here's what you could have won!*"

JK - Jeremy Keith, one of three members of the controversial consortium who acquired The Rams for a nominal £1 each in 2003.

September 26th

It's hardly radical to say that there's a lot nonsense bandied about in internet forums but I stumbled across something today bordering on the bizarre. It started out when I saw that ex-Rams striker Marvin Robinson had joined yet another team, so I decided to have a look how many he'd played for (13 in about 7 years). What I found was a thread on a Port Vale forum (one of the few teams Marv hasn't played for) discussing him. Apparently 34.84% voters thought Marvin was "alright" and 26.3% "absolute shite". Someone then describes him as a "blacky" and a big anti-racism debate ensues (inevitably and rightly). I can only guess that Vale might have been linked with him at some point. I wonder if Marvellous Marvin is aware of these discussions in a tiny corner of cyberspace?

Onto another subject - during the summer the Telegraph reported that 15 year old Jordon Mutch had left Derby's Academy for Birmingham's (thanks, or no thanks, to ex-Rams Academy boss Terry Westley, now at Birmingham). At that time I thought the story was a bit of a space filler but keep your eyes peeled for the name - he's in Birmingham's first team squad tonight for the Carling Cup and could be their youngest ever debutant. (2 minutes after writing this from the BBC website -"Football Association rules have prevented Birmingham from picking 15-year-old Jordon Mutch in their squad as he's too young. You have to be at least 16." The rules must have changed since Lee Holmes made his debut).

(Later in the season, Holmes lost this accolade to Gillingham's Luke Freeman, suggesting that the rules differ between competitions).

September 28th

For anyone reading this before Saturday afternoon likely to have a coupon; I received a "red hot" tip today - Arbroath to win at East Stirlingshire. Don't put your mortgage on it but at 10/11 it might be worth adding to your line. This came from the chap who won a load on East Fife et al a couple of weeks ago. The tip is supposed to be "insider knowledge" rather than his own analysis. (East Stirlingshire lost 6-0 v. bottom of the league last week so something may be afoot).

September 29th

Text received yesterday:

"Half page advert in the Mirror yesterday advertising pay on the day for today's [Birmingham] match against Manu U. No wonder the Golds want out"

The novelty of the Premier League hasn't lasted long there has it? Last year Birmingham blamed their poor crowds on the quality of the opposition (the away fans probably thought the same) but what's the excuse this year? For the record, the crowd was about 3-4,000 below capacity.

Another story in the Daily Mirror claimed that Billy Davies had tried to hype up the players before the Arsenal match by blasting out Tupac in the dressing room. I don't claim to be an expert on Tupac and have only heard some of his pop-rap tracks on the radio sampling Bruce Hornsby and Elton John; which leads to one of two scenarios 1) Billy is trying to motivate the players with a rap/piano combination or 2) Billy is a sufficient connoisseur of Tupac to pick out some darker, harder tracks. I'm sure we'd have beaten Arsenal comfortably with the right music.

Looking at my hit counter, around 5 people read the Journals between me posting my tip on Friday (28th) and Saturday's games; I'd be interested to know if anyone had any joy with Arbroath (they won 3-2 at East Stirlingshire). I planned to have Arbroath, Liverpool and Man U but swapped Man U for Watford at the last minute - gutted.

The full story behind the tip is that the brother of a chap at work (how many times do stories start like this?) works for an independent bookie who, allegedly, has a few high profile clients who owe him cash. As an ongoing arrangement, allegedly, these contacts will tip him off with insider knowledge. Not match fixing but team news, injuries, flu epidemics and the like. The example he gave was when one these people was in a managerial/ coaching post and rang the bookie to tell him the team in question (his team) had injuries and illness and had six men out. My mate's brother rang him with the advice "put yer bollocks on it" and sure enough the afflicted team lost 3-1. Unfortunately, the Observer doesn't print the line-ups for the Scottish third division so I was unable to check if East Stirlingshire had Bruce Grobbelaar in goal. (Checking the spelling on Wikipedia I see that Bruce is 50 next week, Blimey! that makes me feel old).

(The following was written after The Rams 1-1 home draw against Bolton)

September 30th

A couple of points to note from Saturdays game:

1) Billy Davies has never been slow to say when the fans have been impatient and critical (Howard, Mears, tactics, early results etc.). So it should be noted, if only here, that with the Rams bottom of the league, the fans sang his name at length on Saturday.

2) The DJ at Pride Park has finally found a copy of Chelsea Dagger and unveiled this anthem of football celebration 5 seconds after the final whistle of Saturday's slightly disappointing 1-1 draw. (This habit of playing a song immediately irritates me as it drowns out the real atmosphere whether it be cheers or boos. Does anybody really want to hear Take That "Shine" when you've lost 2-1 to Birmingham?)

October 2007

Premier League Table 1st October 2007

		P	W	D	L	Pts	GD
17	Reading	8	2	1	5	7	-9
18	Spurs	7	1	2	4	5	-2
19	Bolton	8	1	2	5	5	-4
20	Derby	8	1	2	5	5	-16

Results:

07.10.07 Reading 1-0 Derby County

20.10.07 Fulham 0-0 Derby County

28.10.07 Derby County 0-2 Everton

October came, the nights were getting darker and the shine of the Premier League had well and truly worn off. There were only three games played in the month due to an international week. All three games in October summed up the Rams situation - turning potential victories into draws, draws into defeats or just simply not turning up at all.

The league table at the start of October showed the Rams as the bottom club but still within one win of the hallowed 17th position. Our goal difference was truly appalling but not to worry; Reading has conceded seven the previous week at Portsmouth so at least there was goals to be had there wasn't there? No, we barely had a shot and lost 0-1.

The following week we played Fulham at Craven Cottage, yet another team with a bad start. We reshuffled the team, dropped last season's top goalscorer Steve Howard to the bench and beefed up the midfield. Fulham had Paul Konchesky sent off on half time and the Rams dominated. I was on holiday in France at the time and kept an ear pinned to the crackly Radio Five coverage. Every time the host said "…and it's over to Craven Cottage" it was another Derby shot, another Derby chance, but the goal failed to arrive. The Rams failed to score for the sixth consecutive away match and the game ended 0-0. It was all a vast improvement though and Billy Davies was even moved to say "I am very confident with the people that we've got, that we can consolidate ourselves in the Premier League". It was our first away point of the season so a step in the right direction but would we ever have a better chance for an away victory?

Derby approached the next fixture, at home to Everton, with some optimism but the game turned out to be a damp squib. As the football phrase goes, Everton completely "did a job" on us and the Rams hardly had a sniff in a 0-2 defeat. Davies swiftly changed his tune about the squad and commented after the game "We just have to keep working very, very hard to get to the next transfer window and add in many areas."

As ever with the Rams, things were starting to rumble off the pitch. Firstly, Chief Executive Trevor Birch suddenly left the club without explanation. The local consortium who owned the club were now faced with all the demands of the Premier League and appointing a bit hitter such as Birch seemed a logical step. Birch certainly had an interesting track record. He had joined Chelsea with the club heavily in debt and helped bring Roman Abramovich to the rescue before moving on to Leeds, where he briefly became chairman to oversee a takeover and avoid administration (at least until the Ken Bates era). He had most recently been Chief Executive of Everton but had lasted only six weeks.

It was never really clear what Birch came to do, what he did, or what he failed to do. If his role was to tie up major signings then he had certainly failed, with Davies repeatedly saying that players had been identified but not delivered. If it was to attract new investment, then he had also failed, with Davies frequently citing the limitations on the budget. Whatever the case, the club announced his departure after only four months in post and added that no further comment would be made.

The name of Adam Pearson was being bandied around by the press at this time. Reports varied and it was not clear if Pearson would just be an investor or if he was heading a consortium to take over. As October came to a close, it was announced that Pearson would take over as Chairman from Peter Gadsby. It was not a takeover but Pearson would be putting in some of his own cash as well as seeking external investment. Pearson acknowledged that things had to improve but said of manager Billy Davies: "Billy has done a magnificent job in getting the club into this position ahead of schedule. He is definitely the man for us and if the worst came to the worst and the club went down, I cannot think of a better man to bring us back up."

The Journals of Derventio - October

October 2nd

Has Billy started the mind games for the Reading match already? We played Reading reserves last night and Davies was reported as saying that Giles Barnes would get a good run out but Earnshaw would "definitely not" play. As it happened Earnie played a full 90 minutes whilst Giles didn't feature at all.

I actually went over for the second half but there were no turnstiles open. Fortunately, a kindly old gent on reception lead me through the inner sanctum, via the trophy room and onto the pitch-side track so I could walk around from the West Stand to East - not something you usually get the chance to do.

The game finished 1-1. The most notable incident was Earnshaw achieving something I can't ever remember seeing at Pride Park - he managed to clear the South Stand with a shot. How did he manage that? He spun and whacked a bouncing ball around the edge of the box; he certainly caught hold of it but didn't get over it particularly well (to put it politely). His Hummer was even more conspicuous in the car park given the lack of first teamers, fat cats and other cars in general. My 5 month old son has a t-shirt with a teddy bear driving a bus and the image always springs to mind when I think of Earnie driving around in his Hummer.

October 3rd

A bit of a typo in Neil Hallam's Trader column last week*, according to his calculations the Rams have conceded an average of 2,857 goals per game this season! Neil has previously classed himself as somewhere between realist and optimist so it's interesting to see that he devoted said column to the likelihood of us conceding 100 goals this season. On a happy note, he points out that although Leicester conceded 112 goals in 1957-57 (sic - you can't expect proof readers on a free paper) they still didn't get relegated. On the subject of Leicester - a Mark de Vries update (see Journals August 16th). After featuring in almost every Leicester game this season, he's been shipped out on loan to Leeds.

It was announced in April 2008 that the Derby Trader, founded by ex-Rams Chairman Lionel Pickering, was to close. Sports Columnist Neil Hallam resurfaced during the summer of 2008 at the Derby Evening Telegraph..

October 5th

I've just cancelled the myspace account basically because I didn't use it a lot and as a result no else really did. I didn't want it floating around in cyberspace hopelessly out of date. I did make an effort one weekend by going to a football forum that befriended me but I made one comment and got a barrage of semi-literate cyber abuse - never again.

October 6th

Text received from Simon:

"I'm in Mark de Vries fan club. His last minute winner bought my treble home" (see October 3rd)

In fairness to de Vries, when I slated him a month or so ago I employed the tactics of proper journalists by glossing over certain facts. When I said he'd been "farmed out to Holland" he was actually playing for Heerenveen for part of it. Looking at the roll call of ex-Heerenveen strikers, he's not in bad company: John Dahl Tomasson (think Milan not Newcastle); Klaas-Jan Huntelaar; Ruud van Nistelrooy; George Samaraas (think £6m); Marcus Allback (again, he must have been good sometime); and current Brazil international Afonso Alves*. Let's get Craig Brown a season ticket!

Alves was to join Middlesbrough for around £13m later in the season.

October 7th

Bryan Robson's latest excuse for Sheffield Utd.'s indifferent start to the season:

"A number of players are not as good as I thought they were when I took the job"

What's the phrase about a bad workman blaming his tools?

October 8th

An article written for the Times Fanzone after The Rams 0-1 defeat at Reading. The title references Derby's away record at the time of writing...

No goals, no points...Part 5

In a weekend dominated by my two least favourite sports - driving and egg chasing, Derby v. Reading was unlikely to grab any headlines. However, for Rams fans it was quite a significant game. After a few high profile hammerings, this was finally a chance to do something, *anything,* away from home. Reading was also a good benchmark. Essentially a team of good Championship players when promoted, Reading proved that it might not take a Sunderland style £35m trolley dash to cope with the Premiership.

In reality, the game provided more frustration and very few answers from a Derby viewpoint. There is no shame in a 1-0 away defeat, just as there was no shame in last weeks draw against Bolton but it begs the question - if we aren't picking up points here, where are they going to come from? Reading didn't look great and didn't apply too much pressure but did have 4 or 5 good chances of which one went in. Derby worked hard and had a fair amount of possession but I can't remember a shot on target. That's the match report.

At the moment we are one of eight clubs with two wins or less. Yes we've conceded a lot of goals but we are still part of a pack - how long we remain so remains to be seen. My brother just sent me a text saying "gutted by today's game. Should have had minimum draw against them. For first time I think we're struggling" and I think that about sums up the mood.

October 9th

The Premier League is widely regarded as the richest in the world, especially when it comes to TV money but just how far are we in front of some of our EU friends? According to World Soccer, Slavia Prague were offered just £24 by Ceska Televize (Czech BBC I presume) for the rights to their Champions League qualifier against Slovakians Zilina. They declined the offer.

On the subject of Europe and money (also from World Soccer), it's no wonder clubs are so desperate to get in the Champions League and not the UEFA Cup when you look at the figures. With the new format of the UEFA Cup, which makes the Cricket World Cup look short and snappy, Tottenham received £2.92m for reaching the quarter finals after playing every team in Europe home and away. When your squad men cost £16.5m* this isn't a great return. Compare that to the economically efficient Bulgarians Levski Sofia who lost all their games in the Champions League group stages but still earned £4.87m, almost twice Tottenham's meagre haul, for a fraction of the effort (literally).

Darren Bent

October 10th

Don't worry that we are probably the last team in Europe to yield either a goal or point away from home this season because as the official website proudly proclaimed yesterday "Pride Park will become the first football stadium in Europe to house a Starbucks outlet". The news that the Baseball

Bar and Grill is being converted into a cafe was accompanied by some 5 star corporate nonsense including: "We feel the presence of a Starbucks store will greatly enhance the experience of visiting the stadium" from our chairman (not as much as three points would Peter) and "...we are actively looking for more partners in the leisure and attractions sector" from Starbucks (is football now "leisure and attractions"?)

The most cringeworthy statement comes at the end "Starbucks Coffee Company provides an uplifting experience that enriches peoples lives, one moment, one human being, one extraordinary cup of coffee at a time". Is it just the British who snigger at things like this?
It's good news for those working at Egg who want to spend three quid on a cup of coffee or fans that have trouble staying awake for 90 minutes. As for me - I shan't be bothering until they introduce the "Jackal's hip-flask Matchday Special".

On the subject of football's increasingly corporate priorities, I read a story today about an Inverness Caley player on a drugs charge after Police "found cocaine placed on a CD" in his car (is that what they call a criminal record? Boom! Boom!). A club statement announced "The club would like to reassure the club's commercial partners, supporters and the public that the club adopts a very firm stance in relation to the use and/or possession of drugs." In that order.

October 11th

My neighbours have just come back from holiday. We were talking about the new Starbucks and I was telling her about their statement (see yesterday). She thought they should make it "one moment, one human being, one extraordinary cup of coffee at a time, thousands of exploited Third World workers".

October 12th

A few bits of correspondence I've received this week:

First up, seemingly everyone's favourite topic: Hummers. The Jackal writes "Jeremy Clarkson driving Hummer on UK Gold...background is General Motors have bought name and made it commercial...60k and it's yours, 3.3 miles to the gallon...and he says it's shit!". £60k? you should get a lower division footballer free at that price. Did we get the Hummer free with Earnie or was it the other way round?

Secondly, Simon on his new favourite topic: Craig Brown (well his favourite topic is actually Mark Ronson but I haven't got enough space here):

"Craig Brown's talking up Scotland's chances on BBC website. No mention of Rams". I suggested that Derby could be linked with Shevchenko and Voronin following Brown's latest European scouting mission. (Scotland are playing Ukraine if you *really* need the joke explaining).

Thirdly, reader John wrote about our ex "Peroxide blonde mistake prone centre back". I'm glad he said "Peroxide blonde" or it could have been one of about twenty. The subject matter was Andrew Davies annual loan-with-view-to-permanent - he's back at 'Boro routine. Are they asking too much or do people realise that he's just not that good?

October 13th

One of the back page stories in the Derby Telegraph this week said how Scotland manager Alex McLeish used the Telegraph coverage of Derby's Scotland internationals to keep tabs on them. I've got nothing against the Scot's but just for a practical joke - I think the Telegraph should start bigging up Bob Malcolm everyday. 6 weeks later - "Malcolm in shock call up for Scotland's crucial clash with Italy".

October 14th

Some schizophrenia on the text by Bob:

21:26 Saturday night "Like it or loath it, that egg chasing result in Paris was the business"

Two and a half hours (and possibly some Sauvignon Blanc) later, without a reply in the interim "Rugby is fucking shit isn't it?!"

My reply on Sunday morning was "Heard my neighbours shouting so looked what was happening. Saw twenty blokes having a man tangle so axed it".

October 16th

It's difficult to avoid all the international hype at the moment but one detail that caught my eye was that the Russia match was kicking off at 4pm. To explain why, I'll rewind a couple of weeks to a tip I received predicting that Arbroath would win (they did), this was followed a week later by a tip on Elgin (they also did). This revealed two things: 1) the tipster (a work mate) knew his stuff; 2) he was in deeper than a couple of quid on the Premier League. Last week at an afternoon meeting, I noticed he was becoming uncharacteristically agitated as it dragged on - this from a man who can stretch a "quick word" over several hours. As the meeting wrapped up around half four, he whispered "thank God, I've got to get my football bets on by 5" which immediately made me think "in which time zone do they kick off at 5pm?" He must have been betting on the Russian 2nd division. As we left, he was telling me about an Albion Rovers victory he predicted the night before, I replied "blimey, you'll be betting on the Johnstone Paints Trophy next" to which he replied "it was bloody Bristol Rovers in that that let me down!"

October 18th

One of the great things about football (or one of the most infuriating depending on circumstances) is how the man on the terraces can see a signing or appointment and think "that will never work" and it doesn't. It makes us all feel like an expert in our own little way. The most recent example of this was Bolton's appointment and subsequent sacking of Sammy Lee. The appointment was questioned in these very pages as long ago as August 23rd with Simon's theory of "the coach is generally the class joker, leading the club farting competitions and the like. Then one day, he puts a suit on and starts asking people to turn up on time - it just doesn't work."* Maybe more clubs should take a leaf out of Scunthorpe's book: after manager Brian Laws' departure to Sheffield Wednesday, Scunthorpe appointed club physio Nigel Adkins as manager. He not only maintained the promotion challenge but won the league at a canter. Scunthorpe fans have since adopted the chant "Who needs Mourinho? We've got our physio!". I'm off on holiday now for a couple of weeks - don't burgle my house. *For more of Simon's insights, have a look in Sunday's Observer or tune into Match of the Day 2 on Sunday night. Possibly the only ex-Cantaloupe pupil to appear in the Observer and on the BBC in the same day.

*The Match of The Day episode was one of a few media requests to Ramspace across the course of the season. After years of being under the football radar in the Championship, Ramspace had approaches from Match of The Day 2, World Soccer, Setanta, Virgin Media, The Times on-line, The Observer and even Nuts magazine. (Much more on Nuts later).

Match of The Day 2 planned to feature some Rams fans at Craven Cottage for the Fulham game and wondered if we were available or knew anyone that was. Neither Chris nor I were going to the Fulham match but our good friend Simon was.

The feature itself was a good few minutes long and featured Simon and some other Rams fans (friends of MOTD2 presenter Adrian Chiles apparently) being interviewed before and after the game by Kevin Day (who Simon would renew his acquaintance with later in the season at the Nuts awards). Simon had to give the BBC his ticket number before the match and when he took his seat, saw a large BBC camera pointing straight at him. This caused some excitement for those in adjacent seats but I think Simon was too modest to say "calm down the cameras are here for me!" The footage screened featured the usual head-in-hands and jumping out-of-seat shots.

The following week Simon was approached by a stranger in a Derby pub who wished to shake his hand before declaring "you said exactly what I think!" which was basically that if we can't win games like that, when are we ever going to win?

November 2007

Premier League Table 1st November 2007

		P	W	D	L	Pts	GD
17	Middlesbrough	11	2	2	7	8	-11
18	Spurs	11	1	4	6	7	-5
19	Bolton	11	1	3	7	6	-7
20	Derby	11	1	3	7	6	-19

Results:

03.11.07 Aston Villa 2-0 Derby County

10.11.07 Derby County 0-5 West Ham

24.11.07 Derby County 0-2 Chelsea

Despite a disappointing October, it was still only goal difference that kept the Rams in last place. Admittedly, the goal difference was horrific but one win would still be enough to take us out the relegation places. In fact, so many teams were struggling that three points would but us level with Fulham who were 14th.

November was as bad as it possibly could have been. The Rams lost all three matches and failed to score for the second month running. The nadir was undoubtedly a 0-5 drubbing at home to West Ham who at the time had a full teams worth of players unavailable.

The Rams looked far better against Chelsea and were unlucky to lose (this was to become an annoying feature repeated against Man United and Liverpool. The Rams would raise their game against a top side and leave fans thinking "if we play like this against the average teams, will be out of this in no time". Unfortunately, we never did).

After the Chelsea match, Billy Davies gave a post match interview in which he claimed, amongst others things, that he had not spoken to chairman Adam Pearson for several weeks. Two days later on November 26th Davies had "left his post by mutual consent". Billy Davies had often divided opinion amongst Rams fans and his departure was no different. However, after recent results such as the West Ham debacle, his post was becoming increasingly untenable.

Paul Ince was the favourite to replace Davies and the Rams approached the MK Dons for permission to talk to him. However, just two days after Davies' departure, it was announced that Paul Jewell had been appointed as the new Rams boss. When asked if he believed the Rams could stay up he replied "Absolutely....We are not adrift. I am sure the players will be disappointed with their points tally at the moment but we have to work together and try to get out of this". The much travelled Stan Ternent was quickly appointed as Jewell's no.2.

In other off the field news, Adam Pearson confirmed that meetings were taking place with various investment groups in America. Details were sketchy as Pearson played his cards close to his chest. One thing for sure was that the "product" Pearson was touting was becoming less and less attractive by the week.

The Journals of Derventio - November

November 3rd

From an email I sent: "fortunately, when you support Derby you can go away for a fortnight and not miss any goals". Now I'm back and about to set off for Villa - let the goal scoring resume.

November 4th

Well, I did try to tempt fate with yesterdays comment but still no joy. Will we score away before Christmas? We have three away games before: Sunderland, Man U and Newcastle. The BBC are digitally remastering Roy Castle* in preparation for the Match Of The Day Christmas special. Visiting Villa Park yesterday, it's amazing to think that it was widely regarded as one of the countries top stadiums until the last couple of years. At first, it was great to be in a "real" ground, close to the pitch, four different stands etc. However, after spending most of half time queuing on the stairs, to join the queue to get down the back, in order to queue on the concourse, dividing to two queues for bogs and food (both still long when the second half resumed) I found myself guiltily wishing for "better facilities" - I've finally been corrupted! It was a similar feeling to saying "I love real old men's pubs I do", then entering one, having a choice of two beers, the bogs are in tatters and the last thing you want to do is speak to, or even look at, one of the fabled "old men". At which point you all say "shall we just go to Wetherspoon's?"

*Foreign readers - trumpet playing presenter of childhood TV staple "Record Breakers". He died a few years ago from cancer, apparently contracted by passive smoking whilst playing his trumpet in working men's clubs. This had the effect of simultaneously power inhaling several hundred fags every night. Not good for the lungs.

November 6th

WARNING - For trainspotters only: a couple of quick "where are they now?s" that I've come across:

Pierre Ducroqc doing a diving header for Strasbourg in France's top division (as seen on Channel 5's French Football round-up).

Mounir El Hamdaoui - has now signed for UEFA Cup qualifiers AZ Alkmaar. A decent step up for saying he had yet another injury ravaged season last year, playing just 7 games for Willem II.

November 8th

It's often said, usually by people like myself, that football isn't as good as it used to be, prices are too high etc., etc. so how about this for a random statistic:

Leeds v. Millwall League 1, 2007 (i.e. third division) attendance: 30,319.
Leeds v. Luton Division 1, 1974 (i.e. future Premiership) third home game after Leeds won the league, attendance: 26,450.

It shows just how many more people go to football nowadays. Of course it might also indicate how fickle Leeds fans can be, considering they got off to a flier this year and had a crap start in '74.

(Info taken from The Damned Utd., the novel based on Cloughies time at Leeds. A brilliant read.)

November 10th (am)

It seems Birmingham are still having a job pulling a crowd. Text from Simon: "Half page advert in The Mirror...you can pay on the gate for the game v. Villa on sunday. Crap club, mind you, the tickets start at twenty five quid"*.

Chatting to Villa fans last week, they couldn't wait for the fixture; the Villa fan summarising the [Villa v. Rams] game in the Observer used two lines on Derby and the rest on the forthcoming derby (without a capital "D"). I hope there are plenty of stewards on duty.

Twenty five quid is not bad though in this day and age. I bought a child's ticket for today's game and it cost me £21. (that's £3 more than Child Benefit incidentally - sorry son, it's beans on toast again). Don't worry - I'm not trying the scam highlighted on the official site (adults entering with kids tickets), it's a legit swap around.

*regular readers will recall Birmingham did a similar trick for that other hard to sell game - Man Utd. at home.

November 10th (pm)

(The following entry follows Derby's humiliating 0-5 home defeat by West Ham)
Last week I did the phone interview for the Observer and was asked several times "are Derby doomed" to which I refused to agree, arguing that we're not adrift and will soon be picking up points. The interviewer, ironically a West Ham fan, must be in stitches tonight.

The day didn't look good from the start; I've got a heavy cold and was ruled out of any pre-match socialising. Then my son's temperature also rocketed and we had to race across town (on Doctor's advice), waiting for an hour to be told that there was nothing to worry about. I made it home long enough to make a flask and dash straight to the game.

At half time we were still optimistic; West Ham had a virtual reserve team out and Derby were so poor that we could only get better. However, pouring my coffee out I realised I'd got the quantities hopelessly wrong: far too much brandy; weak watery coffee; and milk enough to discolour and make the whole thing look like dishwater (and taste like it if Fairy added "Autumn Brandy" to the range). In true British style, Simon drank up with out a word of complaint - but the omens weren't good.

The second half was pure embarrassment. A word of credit has to go to my 5 year old nephew who waited a full 85 minutes before saying "Granddad, can we go home? I don't like this match". He dutifully watched until the end.

Just to cap it all, as the final whistle blew the stadium DJ reached for his newly acquired Hits 2006 album and chose Razorlight's "America" as his drown-out-the-boos song. "What a drag it is, the shape I'm in" - my sentiments entirely J-Bo *(J-Bo - Razorlight singer Johnny Burrell).*

So where do we start after that? Well I'd start by sacking the DVD analyst. You can guarantee an opponent will run through one on one with Bywater at least 3 or 4 times a match (e.g. both Everton goals) but the coaching staff don't seem to have registered this. I'm convinced I could have saved us at least 4 goals over the season armed with just a Betamax and a few Match of the Day repeats.

November 12th

A couple of interesting texts from Simon:

First one: "Friends of [players name removed just in case] have just been telling me that the main focus of training is seven defenders v. five attackers every day"

If our attack was good and defence weak, or vice versa, our weaknesses would become clear within half an hour. The problem is that with our defence and attack being as good, or dare I say bad, as each other, there must be some epic struggles on the training ground but come Saturday the poor chaps don't know what has hit them. I wonder if this is why Tyrone Mears recently claimed he was aiming for an England place? "Eddie Lewis hasn't had a kick all week, I must be brilliant".

Second one: "Ten thousand people [Austrians] have signed a petition trying to get Austria banned from next years Euro's. "Let's not embarrass ourselves" the campaign calls itself as they are ranked 88th in the world and fear a thrashing. Hope our lot don't hear about this"

A great slogan. One for the Rams Protest Group if they ever decide to reform.

November 14th

According to The Mirror, Stephen Bywater is a martial arts expert who spends his spare time "scrapping with his pals", indulging in judo, boxing and jujitsu. That might explain why when I saw him in Morrison's last year he was dressed like a ninja in training - black towelling hoodie, black towelling trackie bottoms and chunky black trainers. Expect to see an immediate decrease in "chocolate wrist" comments on this site. It was Simon who said it anyway - obviously I think he's England's no.1 and just having a bit of bad luck.

November 17th

Here's some figures that might be of interest to some of you who have endured all manner of ridicule, piss-taking and even pity from "fans" of other clubs recently. According to recent research 30 million Brits claim to be "big fans" of certain clubs, with Man Utd., Chelsea and Liverpool the most popular. However, less than half of them (46%) have ever seen their teams play live and another 10% will only do so once in a lifetime.

More interestingly, armchair fans can be so fickle that just over a quarter maintained an interest in their team for three years; even more bizarrely, 2.6m armchair fans will change allegiance five times during their lives!

It's strange to imagine walking into the office and giving it a big "aaaaaaaaagggghhhh!!" to a Man U fan over a Champions League debacle you're not really bothered about anyway - to be told "I don't support them anymore". I don't know how I'd respond to that.

November 18th

Congratulations to ex-Rams striker Lionel Ainsworth. He not only achieved something that the Rams have failed to do all season - score an away goal - but the show-off did it 3 times in 33 minutes during Hereford's 3-2 win at Stockport yesterday. I was going to make some comparison with the Rams away record but mathematically you can't do a lot with "zero". You can't multiply it, divide it or get any percentage from it. Instead, I'll include our home fixtures: what took Lionel 33 minutes has taken us an incredible 1,080 minutes!

Ex-England U19 Lionel was released last summer after three unspectacular loan spells at Bournemouth, Wycombe and Halifax but with two hat-tricks in the bag already this season, don't rule out him "doing an Izale McLeod". Unfortunately, I doubt we'll have a sell-on clause this time.

November 19th

It seems like every idiot feels qualified to have a pop at us at the moment - the latest being unfunny, one-trick-pony, comedian Alan Carr on The Times website (they'll let any riff-raff on there you know).

As the punch line of a jibe about the Disney* rumours he writes "...looking at Derby's recent defeats, 5-0, 6-0 and 4-1, I think they've already got seven dwarves in defence, including Goofy in goal." Firstly, having seven men in defensive positions would be great (height is not an issue, it's all on the floor in the Premiership); secondly, I wouldn't advise calling Bywater "Goofy" seeing as his hobbies include boxing, jujitsu and judo (see Journals November 14th); thirdly, he's got his facts wrong on the scores. Us lose 4-1? Never.

There were rumours around this time of an American consortium called Shamrock Holdings funding a takeover of the Rams. One of the Disney family was a board member, hence several weak puns about Derby being a "Mickey Mouse club".

November 21st

Today's press is full of stories about Billy Davies allegedly having two games to save his job. With Chelsea first up, he's not exactly being set up to succeed (if he's told "fair enough, we'll give you three games" you know he's in trouble, the third is Man Utd away). I'm not even sure who would be the person to "give him two games": Peter Gadsby? Adam Pearson? Ronald McDonald? The Sultan of Brunei?

One argument people have for keeping Billy is the lack of decent candidates to replace him, an argument strengthened by Bolton's appointment of Gary Megson. It's interesting to look at Birmingham though, a club comparable to ourselves (if we had less fans and no history), and also on the verge of receiving substantial foreign investment. Since Steve Bruce departed, they have approached Martini Jol and World Cup winner Marcello Lippi about taking over at St. Andrews. Admittedly both turned them down flat but the ambition shown makes the whole thing look a bit spicier - definitely more interesting than Joe Royle, Peter Reid and the rest of the gang.

In Lionel Ainsworth news (see Journals Nov 18th): for those who didn't clock it, he scored the winner for Hereford last night as they beat Leeds away in the FA Cup.

November 22nd

With the Rams struggling and now England's Euro debacle, it's worth having a moments respite from football before the Chelsea game.

I always like a good bit of marketing spin so how about this from the music world: Why do middle aged rockers Orson always where hats? The PR spin: "to keep a sense of old fashioned Hollywood". The journalist: "it turns out they're just a bit bald".

November 23rd

What a week for Lionel Ainsworth: scored a hatrick last Saturday; scored the winner at Elland Road on Wednesday; signed for Watford on Thursday; no doubt he'll be making love Friday, Saturday and chill on Sunday (a predictable joke but there for the taking). For those who missed it, Watford have signed him on loan with a view to making it permanent when the transfer window opens.

I don't want to be hypocritical as I wasn't up in arms when we released him but it is worth reflecting on. Lionel represented England at both U17 and U19 level and after suffering a few injuries was given his Rams debut by Terry Westley. However, at the age of 18 he was sent on a demoralising tour of the lower divisions before being chucked on the scrapheap. Meanwhile, our own coaching staff, who in an ideal world would be bringing on young talent, are spending time with Macken, Malcolm, Currie etc. trying to polish a turd (as the phrase goes). A year later, they're all back in the Championship (except Currie who's in League 1) with only Lionel on an upwards trajectory. What's the moral of the story? Get Nyatanga back and axe Todd and Griffin (no offence chaps, I'm just thinking of the future).

(Lewin Nyatanga was on loan at Barnsley at this point).

November 25th

(Written after the 0-2 home defeat by Chelsea)

The game was a bit more encouraging yesterday but still no goals. It's funny that Billy can rival any tinker-man when it comes to full-backs and wingers but has stuck with the single striker formation for two months, despite us not scoring once. In contrast, the Miller - Howard partnership yielded a goal blitz in September with us scoring in consecutive home games. Ok, it was only two goals but it was also four points.

A lot of the post match talk surrounded Davies' comments that he hadn't had a conversation with Adam Pearson for 3-4 weeks. By my calculations, that is basically since Pearson became chairman. Presumably, Mr. Pearson has been jetting around pursuing investment. Well, I may have the answer. Can you remember SISU the company who were apparently funding JK's takeover bid? Well, they are now sniffing around Southampton*. Think about it - they were allegedly prepared to pump £40m into us when we were £56m in debt and near the bottom of the Championship. Now we're in the Premier League, a fraction of the debts (if any - I don't know) and money rolling in. Give them a bell Adam, then you can spend some quality time with Billy and stop your carbon footprint rivalling Robert Earnshaw's.

(SISU were later involved in a takeover of Coventry City)

November 26th

(The following entry was written in the wake of Billy Davies' sacking)

King Billy or Silly Davies? I have to admit, I've tended to lean towards the latter but I still felt some sadness over his departure today. In retrospect, the writing was on the wall with Billy's recent public praise of both the fans and his relationship with Gadsby. Contrast this with his post play-off rant and it's clear that Billy realised he was no longer untouchable. No-one can take away his achievements of last year though and it's certainly been an interesting 18 months. It was a shrewd move by Davies to renegotiate his contract in the summer and he's been well rewarded for his efforts.

I know quite a few Rams fans weren't keen on his apparent arrogance and frequent self-congratulation so it's interesting to hear that Paul Ince is the bookies favourite to take over. (Regular readers will remember the self-styled Guv'nor comparing his move from Macclesfield to Milton Keynes to that of Thierry Henry's from Arsenal to Barcelona). Credit where credit's due though: Ince took over the worst team in the country around this time last year and performed wonders. Could he repeat the feat for us?

It's usual when such events occur for Sky Sports to stop a few players driving out the training ground for a quick word. No Derby player stopped to talk. So what did the editor decide was the best few seconds footage of this silence? Earnie driving past in his Hummer.

November 27th

Colin Miller, John Ireland, Pete Williams, John Davies. No, not members of Oasis who aren't Gallaghers but some of the back-room staff who left the club along with Billy Davies. Unemployment figures in Derbyshire saw a definite spike yesterday as a total of 10 people (including BD), the equivalent of a small firm, found themselves unemployed.

Billy Davies often said how the players needed to learn about the Premier League - the truth is that the vast majority of the playing staff have at some time or other been in the Premier League. But as far as I can see, the same cannot be said of the coaching staff. A couple of playing stints by David "Ned" Kelly seem to be the sum of their experience.

Talking of Kelly, what a couple of years for him. Firstly, he gets paid for a whole year by Preston for doing absolutely nothing ("gardening leave"). Then he signs a three year Premier League contract, works a few months of it, then receives a sizeable pay-off (I presume it was sizeable - it was a three year contract after all). The original Ned Kelly must be up in heaven wondering why he worked so hard to make a living.

November 28th

Welcome to Paul Jewell. It was a strange day at work yesterday with those supporting other clubs eager to offer an opinion on Paul Ince, usually with words 4-letters long, and me feeling obliged to defend him - just in case. By the same token I deleted the line "...at least if it all goes wrong we all get to scream abuse at Paul Ince" a couple of days ago as it seemed a slightly negative way to start. I think a few Rams will share Bob's sentiments who texted me to say "Big wide Vs to Pince" as soon as Jewell was confirmed. (U.S. readers "V's" are like the middle finger salute - but twice as good). A quick note for Jewell - in about three weeks a bald Glaswegian will turn up at the training ground. Don't call security - it's Bob Malcolm. (On second thoughts, DO call security).

(Bob Malcolm was on loan to QPR at this time)

November 29th

There must be a flurry of optimism around my family: my brother texted me last night to say money was on for us to stay up at 9/1 and my dad was on soon after to say it was 16/1 for us to stay up and Wigan go down. I had a quick look myself to see that Skybet actually have a selection of "Derby Specials" - most relating to us getting no goals or no points by various deadlines.

I made a point a couple of days ago about our ex-coaching entourage having very little top flight experience between them, so it was good to see Stan Ternent appointed today. There's not a lot in football that Stan hasn't experienced. One unhappy episode I wasn't aware of, until Simon gave me edited highlights of his autobiography over the summer, was when Stan was coach of Chelsea in the early 90s. Working with an arrogant, ill disciplined bunch - lead by Dennis Wise, he was referred to as BBC - Balls, Bibs and Cones. To give you some idea of the quality of the Chelsea team around that time; Frank Sinclair was Player of the Year.

I wouldn't advise any Rams players getting cocky though; after texting Simon to tell him of Stan's appointment he replied: "He's just got off with a charge after he smacked someone at a cricket match in the summer". (Legal note: obviously he didn't smack anyone if he was found not guilty).

December 2007

		P	W	D	L	Pts	GD
17	Middlesbrough	14	2	4	8	10	-14
18	Sunderland	14	2	4	8	10	-15
19	Wigan	14	2	2	10	8	-15
20	Derby	14	1	3	10	6	-28

Results:

01.12.07 Sunderland 1-0 Derby County

08.12.07 Man United 4-1 Derby County

15.12.07 Derby County 0-1 Middlesbrough

23.12.07 Newcastle 2-2 Derby County

26.12.07 Derby County 1-2 Liverpool

30.12.07 Derby County 1-2 Blackburn

When I looked back at the December matches, it was difficult to believe that we only gained one point from the six matches played. If the month had been three minutes shorter (a minute being lost from the Sunderland, Newcastle and Liverpool matches) the Rams would have been four points better off and within a point of our final total. Performances were, on the whole, much improved but all the things that affect teams at the bottom i.e. bad luck, lack of confidence, lack of belief, conceding wonder goals - left the Rams virtually down and out by the end of the month.

In summary:

In Paul Jewell's first match in charge, we more than matched Sunderland in an uneventful game. Sunderland scrambled home a winner in injury time after barely having a shot.

Man United at Old Trafford was always a write off but by all accounts (that's the national press not Derby fan mates!) the score line flattered United, mainly due to an outright dive by Ronaldo in the last minute for the penalty that made it four. On a brighter note, Steve Howard scored the Rams first away goal of the season (it was also Howard's first of the campaign).

Middlesbrough at home was a typical example of the Rams letting down a full house against theoretically beatable opposition. The Rams didn't trouble Boro' at all, although instead of getting a point from a drab 0-0 draw, Boro' won courtesy of a Goal of the Month winner from Tuncay.

Newcastle away could have been the Rams finest moment of the season. The Rams were deservedly winning 2-1 going in to the last minute when an error from Darren Moore lead to a late equaliser. Another two points lost.

Liverpool at home could also have been the Rams best moment of the season. Giles Barnes could have scored the winner in an even game but instead Steven Gerrard did the business for the scousers - again in the last minute.

After a month of "if onlys", Blackburn at home brought another one. Derby started well, went 1-0 up and were then awarded a penalty - the chance for our first two goal cushion of the season. Howard missed the penalty and Blackburn scored twice after some sloppy defending (although Bentley's 25 yarder was harsh punishment). After the month we'd had, the players and fans gave up before half time. The following day Steve Howard was in talks to join Leicester and had played his last Premier League game. Off the field, there was the bizarre episode of Bob Malcolm's drink driving arrest. Malcolm had driven back to Derbyshire from London after a night out and apparently decided to stop for a rest…in the middle lane of the M1.

The Journals of Derventio – December

December 2nd

The defeat at Sunderland yesterday was a real kick in the knackers after a decent day, and a decent performance. It all turned sour at about 10 to 5 but I've just written it all for the Times website *(article featured after this entry).* The day started off well enough, arriving in Sunderland in good time and finding a pre-match boozer whose day job seemed to be an indie club. Cheapish beer and a big screen showing the lunchtime game on the dancefloor. We had a slight problem with the language barrier when Simon asked what cobs they had; after repeating three times the bar maid told him they had normal coke or diet coke. (Non- Derby readers: "cobs" are a.k.a. rolls, baps, barn cakes etc. I don't know what they call them in the North-East but it's safer not to walk into home-fans pub and ask the barmaid about her baps).

When we got to the ground, we had to look for the "pay" turnstile as the Jackal had only decided to come at about 11 O'clock on Friday night. As if by magic, the moment we joined the queue, a lady in front of us brandished a fistful of tickets saying "I just don't know what to do with these".

The tickets were via a player so we all decided to follow the Jackal (as there were other unused spare tickets) thinking that it may be the WAGS section. However, Roy Keane proved to be right about WAGS not fancying Sunderland, with the only evidence of player's friends and family being a sizeable all-male Steve Howard contingent behind us. (One of them revealed he had a bet on Howard for first goal, last goal and Derby to win 1-0. He nearly had a heart attack when Howard headed over at 0-0 with five minutes to go). By the time I'd identified my seat, Simon was already deep in conversation with one of the ticket bearing women. Purely in search of gossip for the Journals, or future freebies, I'm sure. After a bit of ribbing, he later admitted that he'd sat next to the same bloke for seven years at Pride Park and never spoken to him!

I don't particularly want to go into the match as I think I've analysed it enough either in conversation or in my own mind. It would probably suffice to say that the first thing I did when I logged on tonight was to have a punt on Sunderland getting relegated - 3/1 at Stan James.

An article written for the Times Fanzone post Sunderland game:

It's Grim Up North (east)

At about 10 to 5 on Saturday afternoon, I was sat in a now half empty Stadium of Light. Robert Earnshaw was hesitating over the ball and a Sunderland defender nipped in to kick the ball into touch. The corner would see out the match and although a point wasn't great for Derby, it was an improvement on recent form. Inexplicably, the linesman awarded a goal kick. A minute later, Sunderland had scored and the Rams had lost yet again. Five minutes later a group of young teenage Mackems were swarming around a lone Rams fan making his way home. Another five minutes later and a reversal of age, a Mackem "man" was punching a teenage Rams fan, forcing the latter to flee across a busy road. As a mate said "I wonder what they're like when they lose?". An hour later, we were still stuck in traffic on the outskirts of Sunderland. Not a good end to the day.

I realise that the average Sunderland fan will no doubt feel slightly embarrassed by some of the above and these things, unfortunately, do still happen - but I haven't seen it for a while.

How about the match? As all the media have said, it was essentially a Championship standard game. Derby were much improved in terms of commitment and organisation but it was frustrating that we didn't have enough to claim victory against a Sunderland side who were essentially the same as last season, but without the confidence and belief. It's frightening to see that £40 million can have so little impact - what hope is there for the rest of us? A Sunderland fan in The Observer (am I allowed to mention another paper?) said he hoped they would strengthen the defence and midfield in the transfer window. By the time they've done that (and they need to) you're talking a lot of money to stay up - enough to win most European leagues comfortably.

It's been a hectic week for Derby and ending with a point would have been nice but it wasn't to be. With Man Utd away next week, the games are slipping away. A few mates had a flutter on Derby staying up after Jewell's appointment, a touch optimistic you might think. I'm more of a realist - I've just had twenty quid on Sunderland to go down.

December 3rd

From Simon:

"Random fact. Last away goal in Premiership, away to Sunderland 6 years ago, scored by Marvin Robinson".

For those new to the Journals, Marvin got a mention a couple of months ago as he's played for about 12 clubs since that day. Keep plugging away Marv, if you hit a purple patch I'm sure Roy Keane will lash out £5m on you.

December 4th

How's this for demonstrating the gulf in class between the Championship and Premier League; the four players short listed for November's Player of the Month were: winner Chris Iwelumo, Dean Windass, Akpo Sodje and Jonathan Walters. A group of players with 34 clubs between them already.

With due respect, as I daresay they are all solid pro's, I can't imagine any of them making a splash in the Premier League. It's no wonder Championship clubs can charge a king's ransom for anyone who might step up (Chopra, Kamara, Koumas, Jones etc.).

(The player who has most potential to make me eat my words is Jonathan Walters. Before his season he had a truly woeful record but he's suddenly scored a hatful for Ipswich and been called up by Ireland. If I hadn't used the Roy Keane punch line yesterday it would be here.)

December 6th

I was told today that tickets for the Liverpool match sold out within a couple of hours of going on sale. Is that glorious passion by a club having such a dismal season? Or are true fans missing out because of people paying to see the opposition? (i.e. one game a season merchants and local Liverpool "fans" with the on-sale date circled in their diary). I'll give you a clue to my thoughts: using the footballing mentality of taking each game as it comes, I was just working out when to collect my ticket for the 'Boro game...I'll be at home on Boxing Day though *(i.e. the Liverpool match)*. There is possibly some consolation - according to the official Rams website, there are some tickets to the 'Boro game available for a tenner. Now I've just got to get one as the on-line "buy tickets 24 hours" facility doesn't seem to be working outside office hours.

A fellow Rams fan said an odd thing to me today. Talking about the season, he said "Bywater has hardly saved anything this season..." interesting, I thought, it's not often you hear someone slating Bywater (approximately once a fortnight in my case). He then continued to say "...the finishing in the Premier League is just that good". One way to avoid a karate chop to the wind pipe I suppose. (If this has gone completely over your head, read earlier Journals regarding Bywater's pastimes).

December 7th

I managed to get a couple of tickets for the 'Boro game for a Jeff Kenna each and notice the official site are still pushing this - a shame that after the initial frenzy for Premier League tickets we're struggling to shift them for ten quid a piece. It took some working out where I'd be sitting - the Winfield Stand apparently. The area formerly known as the South Stand and ,in a fleeting moment of fans participation, the Ossie End (what happened to this? Did it fade into the background with the Rams Trust?).

The bigger headline i.e. the money spinner, is hospitality packages for the Liverpool match, with the promise: "packages can be tailored to suit individual needs". Sounds good but what can it actually mean beyond a load of food and drink? A half-time lap-dance? Recreational drugs? A Pete Doherty acoustic set? (the latter was previously available only in East London flats for cash payment but as the Editor and I witnessed last Friday at Notts Arena, the poet of Arcadia has gone stadium. We tried to engage a few Forest fans in healthy debate regarding our respective clubs; you'd think it was a good time to put the boot into the Rams but no one wanted to know.)

December 9th

(The following refers to the Man United away game)

It's not often you can lose 4-1 and come away feeling upbeat but today was one of those rare occasions. Coming out for the second half, the big worry was - is this going to be another Arsenal or Liverpool? Especially as we put on another striker and pushed on. If it wasn't for the last half minute and a scandalous dive, we would have drawn the second half 1-1. To a neutral, this would sound like clutching at straws but Rams fans know just how important it was to compete and even better- score. Both players and fans will be ready for next week.

I'm chuffed to bits for Steve Howard scoring his first goal, and the clubs first away goal, at Old Trafford. Ok, as ugly goals go, Iain Dowie could mock this for its lack of beauty but so what? Steve's took more flak than most this year and probably deserved less. A prime example was Villa away when Howard was employed as a lone striker. For 75 minutes or so, every winning header by Howard was greeted with "who the fuckin' hell's that to?" Earnshaw came an as sub and two Howard headers later, Earnshaw has two clear chances. Let's have an Earnshaw goal now and see the famous somersault (although the Jackal claims he celebrates with a firing-a-machine-gun action. Is it either or both? There's only one way to find out).

For those who don't get The Observer, here's an excerpt from Simon's contribution to The Verdict fans panel: "If one player was going to end our drought, it was Howard and it was at our end too. We took the roof off. The guy next to me was irritating me all game, but I ended up hugging him".

December 10th

Only 5 or 6 months ago, Neil Hallam in The Trader claimed that Derby's promotion was on a par with any sporting achievement you could imagine. However, barely a week after Davies' departure, Hallam gives a less favourable appraisal of the Davies era. He begins by quoting Thomas Edison as saying "I have never failed - I have simply discovered 10 thousand things that do not work" before adding "Davies was [...] almost as prolific a discoverer". (I think half of these experiments involved finding someone to play left wing - Smith, Lupoli, Barnes, Fagan, Teale, Currie, Pearson, Lewis, Camara).

To further put the boot in, he goes on to say that Paul Jewell's first job will be "..clearing out an unwanted surplus of under-achievers stockpiled by his predecessor". A harsh (but true) verdict on a bunch who collectively over-achieved last year. Hallam may as well have saved himself a couple of thousand words with another quotation, this time from the Jackal talking about the Davies era: "most people think - thanks for the Play-Offs - now fuck off!".

I do like Hallam's column though. If nothing else, he's the only local journalist to give an opinion on the Rams. He's also up for throwing in the odd bit of gossip and tittle-tattle - something seemingly punishable by death at the Derby Telegraph.

December 11th

Having looked at my list of wide left players from yesterday, you could also add Tommy Smith, (I meant Ryan yesterday) and Jon Stead. I'm sure Bisgaard and Jones have done a turn at some stage as well. One noticeable absentee is a player who has been at the club throughout the Davies era and ironically is one of the few natural wide left players we've had - Lee Holmes. From teenage prodigy to 14th choice left winger. I bet he's gutted Davies has gone.

December 12th

Does Jay McEveley share the same agent as Craig Burley? Not since Burley was here have I known a player quoted so regularly about everything and anything. I don't know whether its press conferences or press releases but just in the last week we've had: "Jay: Stan helped me get on track" (Stan Ternent took McEveley on loan whilst at Gillingham) and "Rooney showed Jay the way" (the two played together as kids).

A quick search on the Telegraph website finds no end of newspaper filler from the scouse Scotsman, such as: "Jay out to ruffle Italian feathers" (talking about Scotland v. Italy), "Sweet memories fuel Jay's cup quest" (the

Carling Cup), "Jay fired up by Cole" (about when he and Andy Cole were at Blackburn) and "McEveley is anticipating a thriller at new Wembley" (self explanatory). There's loads more as well.

I can't wait for him to break his silence on the new fitness coach "He overtook me on the motorway 5 years ago, I knew he was going places..."

December 14th

Logging onto the official website tonight, I was greeted by an advert for the Middlesbrough game accompanied by a picture of Eddie Lewis in full flight. This means either one of two things: whoever does the official website is completely out of touch with the club, the fans and the team; or they are right in the inner circle and Lewis is playing tomorrow. We'll see. The website aren't the only culprits though, the billboards outside the ground regularly run adverts featuring Earnie, yet looking at him for two minutes in a traffic jam is the most you'll see of him.

(In the Neil Hallam article I referred to a couple of days ago, he went through the entire squad, right down to the likes of Miles Addison and James Meredith, about who he'd keep and who he wouldn't. He completely neglected to mention Eddie Lewis. Not intentional I'm sure but it tells a story).

I can't wait until tomorrow, it feels like the first game of the season all over again. The Jackal has stood me up though. Where is he? That's why they call him the Jackal. Keep your eyes peeled - brown hair, medium height, medium build.

Deja vu at Derby

2 months ago, Derby had just put in a promising away performance at Fulham. We were bottom of the league but there appeared to be a glimmer of hope. A new chairman was about to buy into the club and the words "the season starts here" could be heard muttered around Pride Park. This was followed by the dampest of damp squib home performances - a 2-0 defeat to Everton.

Last weekend, Derby put in a credible performance at Old Trafford (forget the scoreline), we had a new manager and are on the verge of a takeover by an American consortium. The words "the season starts here" could be heard muttered around Pride Park. This was followed by a completely demoralising 1-0 home defeat to Middlesbrough. Deja vu? Absolutely, week after week.

To be honest, the defeat didn't particularly sink in at the time; another game, another defeat, we'll start winning sooner or later. (It was possible I was anaesthetised by a pre-match combination of strawberry lager and pear cider. How else do you get your 5-a-day on match day?).

It was only watching Match of the Day on Sunday morning that reality really hit home. Watching Wigan put 5 past Blackburn (remember the Rams have only scored 6 all season) and then seeing Bolton look almost unplayable for spells against Man City (ok they lost but did so in style). If the Rams were to survive, we would be looking to overtake either or both of the aforementioned teams. Not scrape a result in 90 minutes but out - perform them for half a season. It really is not looking good. The same could be said for Middlesbrough, another team in our sights. We weren't particularly outclassed but neither did we deserve much, if anything, from the game. Could we have got a draw? Yes, if we were lucky. Are we likely to score more points than them over 10 or 20 games? I'm usually an optimist but I can't think of any basis to say "yes".

December 16th

Eddie Lewis was on the bench yesterday so maybe the official site do know something. Or maybe not.

December 17th

I see rent-a-quote McEveley's at it again in today's Telegraph with the story "Jay McEveley believes Derby County's miserable run of defeats cannot last much longer and that only a "wonder goal" stopped them from grabbing a point against Middlesbrough."

I suppose there's some logic in that. We lost 1-0. If Middlesbrough hadn't have scored it might have been 0-0 (I can't wait for more in-depth analysis by Jay on Setanta Sports in 10 years time). The goal was after 38 minutes though not 94 as at Sunderland. There's a worrying subtext here, the suggestion that if the opposition doesn't score, we might draw 0-0. If they do, we'll lose. Is a Derby goal really that inconceivable?

December 18th

How the other half live eh? On Saturday the Mirror ran a story about Blackburn's Steven Reid along the lines of "16 months of hell, my injury torment etc., etc."

The same Steven Reid on Radio 1 on Friday morning: Question: What's the last thing you bought yourself? Answer: a Bentley.
I presume he wasn't on Statutory Sick Pay then?

It reminds me of an incident a couple of years ago at QPR. We were standing outside a pub in Shepherds Bush when QPR's reserve 'keeper Chris Day drove past. Simon commented "I feel sorry for him, the way his career's gone". We all looked at each other: we were thrilled at saving a tenner on an advance rail ticket; he was driving through West London in a BMW tank.

December 19th

I see Man Utd.'s Northern Ireland international defender Jonny Evans has been bailed on suspicion of rape. No jokes about Irishman in identity parades shouting "that was her!" please.

December 20th

Preview of the Liverpool game written for Sundays Observer:

"Derby v. Liverpool:

The last time Derby and Liverpool met, Liverpool scored six times in roughly an hour. After five months of trying, Derby's "goals for" column now equals six. Given that we've already scored once this month, it will take something out of the ordinary for Derby to beat Liverpool.

On the bright side, fixture congestion will be taking its toll (on Liverpool, we're concentrating on the league) and football's "silly season" always throws up a few surprises at this time of year. It would be great to base our chances on form or relative strengths of the teams but I'm afraid that's a non-starter at the moment.

Due a big game -

Giles Barnes. Has struggled for form in a struggling team but if he's really worth £5-£7m, he's going to have to show it soon."

The reply was: "Thanks very much, but is there anyone else for due a big game? There is also a preview for Sunday, done by someone else, and they have already chosen Barnes..." *(The Sunday game was Newcastle in which Giles Barnes and Kenny Miller scored)*

Barnes was the obvious choice. Should I go for Bywater? (a clean sheet would do nicely) McEveley? ("Jay: Let's show what we're made of" official website today) Earnshaw? (just simply due a game). I decided to plump for: Kenny Miller: Widely regarded as our top striker but hasn't scored since September.

December 22nd

Text exchange:

Simon on Friday night: "Don't know if its true but I've been told that we've released some more tickets for the Liverpool game today" (regular readers will remember I missed the boat on this game).

Me on Saturday: "Looked on the official website, no mention of Liverpool tickets."

Simon: "[girlfriend] told me that the guy I was talking to last night is a compulsive liar. Wish she'd told me that before I'd sent about ten texts."

Along with thousands of others this weekend, Simon seems to have ended up at a Christmas do talking to all kinds of random cranks. I had a similar experience with my wife's work crowd. I turned up sober and soon had my ear bent by a beered-up chap telling a truly heart-wrenching story about a colleague who had discovered his wife (and mother of their three kids) was having an affair (the afflicted party, also there, was evidently in tatters). He concluded by saying "at the end of the day mate, it's Christmas. And it's his problem. Cheers!". (A flavour of Christmas in Derby for absent readers).

Back to the subject of Sunderland; I'm no Buddhist but Sunderland's karma seems to be catching up with them rather quickly. I haven't seen the contested goal by Reading at the time of writing but it appears to be making the headlines (I've seen last weeks disallowed goal against Villa and it seemed [bouncing-shoulders-laughter] rather harsh.) I don't recall

Sunderland appealing for justice when Fulham had a legitimate second disallowed against them (and subsequently drew) or when the linesman made an erroneous decision in the build up to the Mackems winner against us. To quote the Jackals favourite Libertines lyric: "Fuck 'em!"

December 25th

Happy Christmas!

Thanks to everyone who reads the Journals and thanks for the occasional email that I get - let's have a few more in the New Year!

I hope you occasionally read something you hadn't already heard or have the odd chuckle. Even though there's no commercial element to it at all, there wouldn't be much point if no one ever read it - Up The Rams!

December 27th

A desperately disappointing end to the two Christmas fixtures. If this was a couple of months ago, we could say "at least we won't have a problem competing at this level" but I think it's too late for that now. To make matters worse I had £2 on us to beat Newcastle 2-1 at 40/1.

It was nice to see Rent-a-Quote on the scoresheet *(against Liverpool)* as he's an Everton fan (as he told us in the Telegraph before the game). In return, his media profile rose to a post match interview on Match of The Day.

Talking of Match of The Day, one of the panellists after the Newcastle game was Championship specialist Billy Davies (remember him?). Even looking at it objectively, it's an odd concept to have someone with one of the worst Premiership records ever acting the expert. The subject of Newcastle conceding early goals came up and he was asked, as a manager, how to prevent this. His long answer concluded that professional players should know that they have to concentrate - that's "do nothing" then. The next question was how Derby could improve their situation - with a wry smile, Billy said we needed to bring some players in during January. In fairness to Billy, he didn't have a bad word to say about the Rams.

December 28th

Text exchange today:

Me: Sky Sports news - Bob Malcolm charged with drink driving

Simon: They should have tested Silly Davies when we signed him.

We don't like to stereotype people here at Ramspace (for example, you wouldn't hear us singing - to the tune of "Hey Baby" - "Heeeeeeey Scousers, I wanna knoo-o-o-ow where my stereo?") but Bob Malcolm has single - handedly set the image of the shaven-headed Glaswegian male back ten years. Was the City of Culture all in vain Bob?

December 30th

In a novel I got for Christmas, one of the characters pretentiously discusses the phrase "déjà vu" by saying the "vulgar use" is to describe experiencing something you've already experienced; whilst the proper use is to describe something you haven't experienced before but feel you have. The Blackburn game was a bit of both: it felt as though I'd seen it all before. However, looking at the "proper" meaning: I hadn't already seen the game but at 1-2, I had a good idea of the outcome. I don't think I was the only one. With a few minutes to go and only one goal in it, Derby were pressing on and won a couple of corners. Rather than urging on the equaliser, Rams fans were streaming out of the ground. We didn't play particularly bad but levels of expectation seem as low as ever - the Liverpool and Newcastle games have taught us that we can play well but good things just don't happen to us.

The only notable point of the day was the Jackals introduction of hot cider. Somehow, his household had ended up with a surplus of whiskey, so we decided to reduce the stocks, accompanied by some food provided by yours truly. After some Irish Coffees, we then tried the internet sourced recipe of whiskey, cider and cranberry juice (in lieu of crème de cassis), served hot. Sounds dodgy but perfect for a winters match. Unfortunately we forgot to invite Bob Malcolm round for a couple of Jackachinos - he could have given us a lift to the ground. (Bob Malcolm was pictured on the front page of the Telegraph a couple of days ago - my mate Bob's dad asked "who's he?", a genuine "Who are ya!")

January 2008

Premier League Table 1ˢᵗ January 2008

		P	W	D	L	Pts	GD
17	Sunderland	20	4	5	11	17	-19
18	Wigan	20	4	4	12	16	-16
19	Fulham	20	2	9	9	15	-14
20	Derby	20	1	4	15	7	-35

Results:

02.01.08 Bolton 1-0 Derby County

12.01.08 Derby County 0-1 Wigan

19.01.08 Portsmouth 3-1 Derby County

30.01.08 Derby County 1-1 Man City

Transfers:

IN	OUT
Laurent Robert (Free)	Steve Howard (£1.3m)
Emmanuel Villa (£2m)	Andy Griffin (£300k)
Danny Mills (Loan)	Matt Oakley (£500k)
Robbie Savage (£1.5m)	Jon Macken (undisclosed)
Hossam Ghaly (Loan)	Stephen Bywater (Loan)
Miles Sterjovski (undisclosed)	Lewin Nyatanga (Loan)
Roy Carroll (Free)	
Alan Stubbs (Free)	

January began with The Rams most definitely adrift at the bottom of the table. Transfer activity started immediately with Steve Howard sold to Leicester so quickly that he was able to play for his new team on New Years Day. The Rams rounded off the Christmas period with yet another last minute disaster - conceding a farcical last minute goal in an uneventful match at Bolton. In the last few weeks alone, five points had been lost in the last minute. If added to the Rams' final total, we would have finished on 16 points, one more than the previous worst Premier League tally.

The Wigan game included just too many new signings but Portsmouth away was a small improvement despite the result. The month ended with a deserved 1-1 draw against Man City and once again we were optimistic of getting a few points on the board.

Jewell had been building up to the transfer window and he certainly went about his business with gusto, striking 14 deals in total (plus some other low-key loan-outs). The eight players that arrived included a few gambles but collectively had far more top level experience than our existing squad. Unfortunately, I never saw Danny Mills play, being on holiday for both his appearances. An injury meant that we were not only denied Mills' presence for the remainder of the season but the Premier League declined our request to cancel his loan, meaning that our quota of loan players was filled.

The most controversial signing was undoubtedly Robbie Savage, especially as he was immediately installed as captain.

No one held out any genuine hope of surviving now but the squad looked much improved and most Rams fans were optimistic that we would be able to salvage some pride from the season.

January also contained a brief Rams F.A. Cup run. After scraping past Sheffield Wednesday on penalties at Hillsborough, the Rams were humiliated by a 1-4 home defeat by Preston who were themselves struggling in the Championship. The game was notable only for Robert Earnshaw's first competitive goal for Derby.

Off the field, the takeover of the club was completed at the end of January, with American firm General Sports and Entertainment (GSE) fronting a group of investors from around the world. Adam Pearson remained on the board as Chairman of Football with Peter Gadsby and Don Amott remaining as non-executive Directors.

January 1st

I was a bit surprised to see Howard shipped out so soon. I was having a conversation with my dad earlier in the day about the pros and cons of keeping various players and Howard was one of those we concluded we should probably sell - the rationale being that he'll be turning 33 next season so probably wouldn't be the best bet to lead us back to the Premiership. If we did come back, he wouldn't be leading the line in 2009. To me, the sale of Howard signifies the end of an era as much as Gadsby's abdication or Davies' departure. Now let's get on with 2008.

For the record, I think some of the stick Howard has taken this season has been harsh. Our goals conceded column is equally as woeful as the goals scored but if you asked any Rams fan who was to blame, the answer is likely be "the defence" not Bywater, Griffin, Mears, McEveley, Todd, Davis, Moore or Leacock (the midfield, most notably Pearson have also been guilty). Some, if not most of those listed, have been multiple offenders and have struggled at least as much as Howard this season. Ask any Rams fan who is to blame for our lack of goals, the chances are they will say "Howard". I suppose it's the occupational hazard of being a striker: you are almost always judged by goals and judged as an individual.

A final Steve Howard story from his Wikipedia entry - quite apt after the Blackburn match:

"Howard was almost sacked from Luton in late 2001 after an incident during an away game against York City. The Hatters had been awarded a penalty, and Steve grabbed the ball from the designated penalty taker and promptly missed. However, an infringement was noticed and the penalty was ordered to be re-taken. Against the protests of the senior players and the management team, Howard once again grabbed the ball and stepped up to take the penalty, missing once again. He was substituted immediately afterwards and he walked straight into the changing rooms."

January 2nd

Whatever would journalists do without the internet? Yesterday, I was on the net and saw that we were signing Emanuel Villa, I hadn't heard of him so had a quick look on Wikipedia. There wasn't much on there: his age, height and previous clubs with stats only for his last two. Lo and behold, today's Derby Telegraph ran a back page story about the signing and guess what they'd unearthed about Manny V? "The 25 year old, who stands 5ft 11in, has hit 10 goals in 28 appearances...etc.". It then lists his previous clubs, with stats only for his previous club. Whatever happened to doing some proper research?

The lazy journalism continues (Bolton have just scored so this may take a bitter turn), by saying that Villa will be the third Argentinean to play for the Rams after Fuertes and Carbonari. I make it the fourth - don't forget Zavagno, the most recent of the lot. After all of ten seconds research, I can reveal that Zavagno is now playing for Pisa in Serie B.

January 3rd

A "Season so far" article I wrote for this Sunday's Observer:
What do you make of the season so far?
It's been worse than we could possibly have imagined.
Where will you finish and why?
Bottom. In my view, Billy Davies underestimated the Premiership, sending out players and systems that fell woefully short. He signed 10 players in the summer but none have had an impact [*I had a 120 word limit for the whole piece so had to go with the "broad brush" analysis*]. We have been hammered by some

good sides but have also lost to a lot of mediocre teams. We have competed better under Jewell but the ship hit the berg months ago.

Who has been your star man?

No-one really but Oakley and Miller have been better than others.

Who if anyone has been the boo-boy, or perhaps the most disappointing player?

Earnshaw has been a massive disappointment. Our record signing and best hope for a dozen goals but neither manager has played him and he's still yet to score.

Champions?

Arsenal

Going Down?

Sunderland, Bolton and...possibly us. [*Bolton were chosen ahead of Wigan or Fulham on the assumption that Anelka will be sold and according to the papers will be replaced by two blokes from West Brom*]

The chap at the Observer replied "Thanks very much - very honest of you".

Well I couldn't exactly big us up could I!

I'm away for the weekend so updates in a few days.

January 8th

I've only been away a few days and so much activity! The same happened last year when I was in India and got a text from my brother with news of 4 signings. I won't discuss the signings too much as I suppose that's happening in the forums but it would probably suffice to say that Jewell and Pearson are doing something very different to what Davies and Birch did (or didn't do). There's a whole new world outside Scotland and ex-Preston players. Saying "we've got Robbie Savage and Laurent Robert lined up" to prospective signings is a bit more impressive than "Griffin and Eddie Lewis are almost in the bag" - you can just imagine "erm...I'll leave it thanks mate". *(my optimism regarding Savage and Robert is laughable in retrospect).*

I went to Hungary to stay with a Watford fan I know. I was idly playing with a Watford coaster when a question occurred to me: "Why are Watford known as the Hornets when their badge is some kind of Moose?" Apparently, the badge (a stag) is the emblem of Hertfordshire and "the Hornets" was a Graham Taylor stunt akin to Sunderland christening themselves the Black Cats a few years ago. A bit of useless information for you.

My Dad bought me a copy of The Observer to see how the "season so far" article turned out. After reading it - it looked like I'd been a bit harsh on Earnie. I've seen the feature before and for the "boo boy" category, I was going to write something like "no one has been singled out, Rams fans aren't like that, who do you think we are, West Ham? etc." but I re-read the question and it was "boo boy..or perhaps the most disappointing player". The natural choice was Earnie: record signing, hasn't played, hasn't scored, disappointing to say the least. The printed version simply said "boo-boy", evoking images of me chucking pies at him whilst he's warming up and dragging 50p pieces down the side of his Hummer. A big picture of Earnie in the paper emphasised the point. So in case you're reading Earnie, I didn't mean any malice. If you see me crossing the road when you're driving to the ground, don't pretend your brakes are playing up.

January 9th

(Written in reference to Derby's loan signing of Danny Mills)

You read it here first. From the Ramspace "New Chief - Adam Pearson" article:

"One last word – Pearson lives in Harrogate [...] Amongst his neighbours are Mick McCarthy and Danny Mills. I'm off to start the rumours…"

I was talking to the author, A Hull Fan At Work, about Danny Mills only a week ago and he wasn't particularly complimentary about him. However, I asked him with renewed interest today and a lot of it seems to relate to the Charlton v. Hull game this season. Having recently been on loan at both clubs, Mills whipped himself into a frenzy, culminating in him getting sent off and offending all and sundry: Hull because he acting like a psychopath; Charlton because they were down to 10 men; and probably Man City because he came back three weeks early from his loan excursion (whether Sven allowed him to rejoin training is not known). However, he assured me today that had Mills been at Pride Park all season, opposing strikers wouldn't have been waltzing through the Rams defence in such comfort- and that can only be a good thing. I'm not suggesting that there's ever any merit in getting sent off but the fact that we haven't had anyone red carded this season (especially in the current climate) is probably indicative of the lack of passion in our play - even during some of our horror shows, no one has lost their rag.

January 10th

If you ever thought Sunday supplements were filled with any old crap sandwiched between lucrative adverts, how about this for filler from Sunday's Observer Sport magazine:

"20 Footballers who should have been characters in 19th-century novels"
At number 2 we have - "Giles Barnes - Dogged inspector of farms such as Brambles'*", followed by ex-Ram "Tom Huddlestone - Doughty yeoman, not a malicious bone in his body"
I'm sure it was all very funny in the office on a Friday afternoon. If you went to Public School.

*No.1 is "Titus Bramble - Sturdy farmer wrongly accused of a crime of passion." I think the News of The World wrongly accused Titus Bramble of a crime of passion a few years ago. This one involved several other footballers and took place in a London hotel rather than a country farm. Allegedly.

Still with The Observer, I had to smile at the Sunderland fan in the "Season so far" article who said they could do with strengthening the defence (they signed 5 in the summer - Halford, Anderson, McShane, Higginbottom, Harte), a midfielder (just the 2 in the summer - Etuhu and Richardson) and a striker (4 signed in the summer - Chopra, Cole, O'Donovan, Jones). I feel a "Manage The Mackems" article coming on...watch this space.

January 11th

It could be the dawning of a new era tomorrow *(Wigan at home with several new signings)* - I can't believe I'm not going to the match! Instead, I, along with a few people often mentioned on these pages, will be watching Barcelona v. Murcia at the Nou Camp in honour of the editors stag do. Wigan at home seemed as good a game as any to miss when it was booked several months ago but our thoughts will definitely be in Derby come 3pm. (In case you wondered why I've had two holidays in such a short time - the wife and child have gone to the in-laws for a fortnight).

Jagger hasn't told us who will be captain yet but I know where my money is. It's highly likely to be a Jewell signing who is here for the long haul - flowing blonde hair and a Welsh accent aren't a prerequisite but could be a feature.

January 14th

One reason why I tend not to write too much about forthcoming matches is that 1) it soon becomes obsolete and 2) It can make me look stupid (and usually does). So opening the software to write this tonight, I cringed to think that people had read the Journals on Sunday and today to be greeted with excitement about the Wigan game.

A few of us decided to go to the Sheff Wednesday replay tomorrow in a moment of enthusiasm on Saturday afternoon. After Wigan scored, the subject wasn't raised for a couple of days but revived again this morning. Now we've found out no new players will be on display but we're *still* going. Passion for the club or ambulance chasing? (I could have sworn I heard Bob saying "shall we not bother?" in the background when I rang the Jackal about pick-ups and told him about the team news).

I just wonder if we'll be able to get a team together? By my calculations we've got 9 less players available than we had at Friday lunch-time: Oakley and Grifter have been sold; Holmes loaned out; Savage, Villa, Ghaly and Robert are ineligible; Davis suspended; and now Benny Fill has followed his Presidents example and gone for talks in the Middle East *(Feilhaber's proposed transfer to Maccabi Tel Aviv was to fall through)*. We weren't exactly flush with players in the first place without all the injuries. I'd like to think we may see some youngsters but in reality it will probably mean starts for Macken, Fagan, Jonno, Eddy and Lewis.

January 15th

I'd assumed there would be loads of tickets available for the Sheff Wednesday game but I checked the official website last night and over 3,000 had already been sold; we were down to the last few. My dad raced to Pride Park this morning to get a handful only to find out a couple of hours later that the game had been postponed. For the second time running, my previous entry has soon become irrelevant.

It probably did me a favour bearing in mind I've got a fortnights housework to do before tomorrow. I thought instead that I'd steer clear of the Rams and write about the Barcelona trip but that will have to wait a couple of days as 1) I've got too much housework to do and 2) Publishing holiday stories before you've had chance to tell your spouse probably isn't wise.

January 16th

I had a bit of a moan at the start of the season about how there had been a massive unpublicised rise in match day ticket prices. Most fans only discovered this when trying to buy tickets for the Portsmouth match and suddenly realising why a cash machine had been installed at Pride Park. Prices were billed as "starting from £29-£30" but the snide bit was that no games fell into that category with Pompey, Birmingham and Bolton all being classed as "Gold" forty quidders.

It's only fair then, to mention that ticket prices seem to have gone down in a similarly stealthy fashion, with all recent home games including Tottenham and Man City being in the lowest category. I don't know if it's Adam Pearson's influence or simply a victory for common sense but I for one will be a few quid better off.

January 17th

Trying to explain the Savage signing to a non-football fan makes you realise how football has a moral code all of its own (for the record I was in favour of signing Savage). In his Trader column, Neil Hallam says "...the mere mention of this vexatious character's name is sufficient to make me hold my nose." and "I have always regarded him as a particular virulent species of "anti-footballer". I've checked my dictionary and I don't think Hallam likes him.

To me Savage is a wind up merchant who has indulged in more than his fair share of gamesmanship - basically a pantomime villain. However, I bet Sunderland's interest in Savage caused more moral outrage than the signing of alleged rapist Jonny Evans *(charges against Evans were eventually dropped)*. Some footballers get up to all kinds of despicable antics: alleged rape; drugs; excessive drink (the objection to the last two being that we pay them to be in peak physical shape); adultery; wife beating; and just being plain obnoxious and complete idiots - but are we really bothered if it's off the park? I wonder if Hallam and others would object to drink driver Bob Malcolm turning out on Saturday for the Rams (not forgetting that Malcolm allegedly drove 130 miles under the influence, endangering hundreds of lives as he went)? Well, they probably would, but only because he's completely shit. As far as I know, the only life Savage has endangered is his own by winding up 40,000 fans most weeks.

Vaguely related, I was talking to A Hull Fan At Work about ex-Radio1 DJ and TV Presenter Andy Kershaw. Seems like a decent bloke. Apparently, he's just been banged up for breaching a restraining order placed for harassing his ex-wife. On top of that he's a raging alcoholic who has been ordered to dry out...but still, how can he not be a nice bloke listening to all those sunny African beats? Next time you hear him on the radio playing World Music and think "I don't really get this", just remember, he's probably sat at his decks absolutely trolleyed.

January 18th

Right, the Barcelona trip. Picture the scene, you're sitting on a plane, dozing off at half seven in the morning when you hear a voice booming down the aisles "Craig Fagan is a piss-poor man's El Hadji Diouf!" We were off. (Simon's rationale being that Fagan fails to either wind up opposing defenders or score goals. He probably doesn't spit straight either).

I won't write a long vanity piece but I'll try to pick out a few highlights and observations:

We went to the Nou Camp on Saturday to see Barcelona v. Murcia. You'd be surprised at the number of English voices on the way to and from the match. Barcelona won 4-0. The thing that struck me was that everything was passed to feet by both sides. I suppose you can see that on the telly but seeing it live, I can't stress enough how bizarre it would have looked for a defender to lump the ball forward. There were very few Murcia fans to be seen; one I do remember seeing was carrying a pig skin of booze that he must have looted during the civil war, it made Jackals hip flask look like a shot glass.

After the match it was back onto the town. A few drinks, a lot of laughs and a lot of people agreeing to do the Pride Park 10k run. No one was quite sure how far this was in reality; Jackal was threatening to start his training soon whilst Simon maintained a few star jumps beforehand would be sufficient. A few hours later in a club, me and Simon reflected that if our "jogging on the spot" dancing had forward momentum, we would have been in Valencia by now, never mind passing Frankie and Benny's.
I learnt one thing that night: dance music sounds better through strobe lights and dry ice at 5am in Barcelona than it does on Radio 1 when you're in a hurry to get from Ilkeston to Ripley in the afternoon.

The walk home afterwards was an obstacle course due to an abundance of African prostitutes with strict sales targets and aggressive marketing methods. I tried to emphasise that I wasn't interested by saying "I'm married" and showing my wedding ring. I don't know if this was interpreted as displaying some "bling" (it's a simple gold band) but I was chased up the Ramblas and kicked up the arse in a scene resembling a soft porn Benny Hill sketch.

We did do some sight seeing. Me and Simon met Jackal and Bob at Sagrada Familia. We had a coffee and debated whether or not to go to Sheff

Wednesday. As we walked to the taxi rank, we saw a massive unfinished Cathedral over our shoulder.

All in all a great trip and by tea time on Saturday, we weren't so gutted about missing the Wigan game.

(My wife's just slated me by saying "is anyone really interested in your holiday?" so I'll sign off).

January 20th

Column written for the Times Fanzone after the Portsmouth match:

Jewell's Quiet Revolution

Billy Davies signed in excess of 20 players during his spell as Rams manager. The team that faced Portsmouth on Saturday, less than three weeks after trading began in January, contained only four of them. It would probably have been two, had we completed other deals on the table. It is safe to say that Jewell did not like what he saw when he took over at Pride Park. There were a couple of injured players that may have featured but Jewell could make no greater statement of intent than he did when sold last seasons Player of the Year Steve Howard and captain Matt Oakley ("it's no secret that I was close to Billy" Oakley said as he departed).

So what does this tell us? Firstly that Davies completely misjudged the standard of the Premiership. It took several months of "this team will get better" and "I'm confident we will start winning matches" before Billy suddenly changed tact and announced that we needed 6 new players. Secondly, it's not as difficult to sign new players as Davies would have us believe (although the blame should probably be directed towards ex-Chief Exec Trevor Birch and praise towards new Chairman Adam Pearson). Saturday's match hardly seems worth a mention - another Derby defeat (to another successful club who can't even muster a 20,000 gate, as we astonishingly continue to pack in over 30,000 every week) is probably as boring to read about as it is to write about. On a positive note, that's now three goals scored in our last three away games! Remember we didn't get our first until December 23rd.

So where does this leave Derby now? As far as I can see, we've got the longest pre-season ever. A chance to bed in new players and for Jewell to start building a new team. We're scoring the odd goal nowadays and conceding a few less (with the exception of yesterday) - we still live in hope of something to smile about.

January 21st

A few days ago, I wrote about how ticket prices had quietly come down by classifying all recent games in the bottom "Silver" category. On top of this, we've had £10 tickets for the Middlesbrough match and deals for Sheff Wednesday and Wigan packages. With this in mind, I was intrigued to read the following in a Hull City fanzine:

"Paul Duffen and his mates [Hull City's new owners] are witnessing first hand some of Adam Pearson's sales techniques. I would predict upwards of 4,000 free tickets were available for most home games last season while Duffen was considering an offer for the club. Excellent marketing by Pearson, the ground looks full, earnings potential massive, big club, big asking price".*

Let's hope the American takeover drags on a while, I've already saved at least 50-60 quid on matchday prices. If things on the pitch continue, they'll probably be paying me to turn up by Easter.

(*My source was the paper version of the "City Independent", the website is www.cityindependent.net)

January 23rd

I see Craig Fagan took a few steps to being a slightly better man's El Hadji Diouf last night (see Journals 18th Jan). No, not by displaying some dazzling skill but by his crowd-incensing celebration in front of the Spion Kop after netting Derby's winning penalty *[against Sheffield Wednesday in the F.A. Cup]*. His credibility immediately shot up with 3,000+ Rams fans.
Step 2 - score a real goal.

January 24th

Something I've noticed during this transfer window is the lack of players moving from the Championship to the Premier League. From memory the list is basically Marlon King and a couple of teenage full backs. During the last transfer window, three clubs fished from this particular pool of talent more than anyone else: Us (Davis, Earnshaw, Price. Lewis, Griffin and Mears also spent most of last season there); Fulham (Baird, Cook, Bouazza, Kuqi, Healy, Kamara) and Sunderland (Higginbotham, McShane, Etuhu, Chopra, Jones). Coincidently, the bottom three teams are currently us, Fulham and Sunderland.
(A Fulham fan in the paper recently claimed Kamara was, pound for pound, worse value than the infamous Steve Marlet).

Other facts which may or may not be related: the third promoted club, Birmingham, signed no Championship players. Steve Bruce was the only manager of the three to have managed in the Premier League before.*
Steve Bruce subsequently left for Wigan. Birmingham were subsequently relegated.

January 26th

It looks like the American takeover is going ahead. I wrote a few days ago about ticket prices being lower of late and speculated that maintaining 30,000+ crowds was healthy for the takeover. I don't want to get into conspiracy theories but I couldn't help noticing that now this seems to be sorted, the prices for the Sunderland match are out and it's a Gold game! (i.e. a higher bracket than Tottenham and Man City). I'd be intrigued to know how these things get decided. More confusingly, the default price for a Gold game is now listed as £37 rather than £40, I presume this is building in the on-line discount?

Those of you with season tickets will probably have little interest in the last bit other than to feel pleased that you don't have all this hassle. The Jackal and I were trying to work out what to do for the Spurs game last night. We need to return Man City tickets as some freebies have come up so we thought we'd do a straight swap. My dad's 60 now though so we might as well buy an O.A.P. and swap with his season ticket, Simon's on holiday so we could use his season ticket, Bob might be in corporate in which case his ticket could be spare but my brother will take his son, so we might as well buy a kids ticket...my head was absolutely spinning by the end of all this. Luckily the Jackal is a master of working out such complications - usually solved by "I'll get the tickets, if you give me a fiver, buy me a pint and pay for my 5 a-side, we're all square...are you fucking thick or something?".

January 27th

A couple of weeks ago I commented how we hadn't had anyone sent off this season. It now looks like I've put a curse on us now with two in the last fortnight. Fortunately I didn't go to the Preston game yesterday as it was the editor's wedding. In his role as an usher, Bob made sure all the guests' needs were met, with a discreet "0-2" gesture during the vows.

I went to the ticket office today and whilst there asked the young lad serving how games are categorised (see yesterday's Journals for the relevance of this) or more to the point why Sunderland should be "Gold". After being as surprised as I was, he came out with the unlikely and slightly bizarre theory of "I think they decide if it's going to be a good game or not and the Sunderland game will probably be better than the other two (Tottenham and Man City)". I think his theory was loosely based on the likelihood of us winning. Maybe he has a point, at £15 someone obviously realised the Preston game would be crap!

January 28th

Having read excerpts from the Press Conference and the open letter from Andy Appleby, I have to say that I'm on board for the takeover. The new men are said to be experts at marketing but even so, it was good to see no mention of "soccer" or "franchise". My reasons for optimism are as follows: 1) They have a track record of success in sport (according to their on-line biographies - my C.V. is equally as impressive) 2) They are professionals in their field rather than someone's vanity project. 3) The Chief Exec is relocating from the US so they evidently mean business. 4) They will only make money if we have success on the pitch. All in all potentially more exciting than turning into Coventry or Wolves.

One question that keeps cropping up is why investors would want to get involved in the Rams and how they would ever make money? I've already heard people on the radio saying ticket prices will go up. Personally, I can't really see this happening. Even if you put £10 on each ticket (highly unlikely) the extra revenue over a season would barely buy you a Chopra or Kamara, never mind pay his wages. However, if you play Man Utd. and can get a slice of 50m Chinese pay-per-viewing, a few million Indians downloading the goals to their phones and half of Malaysia watching it over the internet on contract then it could well be worth more than my tenner. One thing is for sure, we've got to get back into the Premier League. I was interested to see that Andy Appleby of GSE is from Michigan. According to my stats for the Journals, Michigan is also home to one of the regular readers. Coincidence? God knows what impression he'd get of Rams fans from this. *(Hits from Michigan dried up around this time!)*

January 29th

I was talking to the editor a couple of days ago about potential articles and we were saying how we didn't want to go too far down the road of slagging off the current squad. Firstly because it's generally a negative thing to do and not a good way of supporting the club; and secondly because you live in hope that the players will turn good at some point and don't want to be hypocritical or have egg on your face.

With that in mind:

1) You've probably all read the Bob Malcolm story: twice over the drink driving limit, decided to drive from London to Derbyshire, then decided to have a kip in the middle lane of the M1. There's no point me adding any commentary to this (although I think the "give the guy a break" comment by someone on the Derby Telegraph website might be a bit generous).

2) We can now safely say that Jon Macken wasn't a particularly good signing as he joins the exclusive club of Rams strikers never to have scored. Full analysis to come when I get round to the *[Ramspace article]* Departure Lounge.

January 30th

I've been off work today, for possibly the first time ever, with a stomach bug. I feel like a colleague who said to me last year "I can't understand it, I've usually got a stomach of iron. I've eaten all over the world and had no problems. Prague, Czechoslovakia, everywhere".

Whilst at home I've taken the chance to read a book about corruption in football (Broken Dreams by Tom Bower. As Simon said "plenty of ammo for the Journals in there"). So far it has been mostly about Venables and

Bates but our friends down the road also get a few mentions. One particular story involves Forest's then assistant manager and Cloughie's partner in crime (quite literally) Ronnie Fenton. Forest are signing a few Scandinavians and for one particular transfer (Toddy Orlygsson) Fenton is dispatched to collect £45,000 in cash from a trawler moored at Hull. This is not just alleged but stated as fact.

Now, I'll begrudgingly admit that Forest enjoyed some moderate success around that time. Fenton spent six years as Cloughie's assistant. Most assistants in that position would eventually either take the reins themselves or become chief at another club. What did Fenton do? He retired to Malta when the F.A. enquiry started.

January 31st

Before last nights match *[against Man City]*, the Jackal told me that according to Sky Sports, Darius Vassell was on 49 Premier League goals and looking for his 50th. My first thoughts were that this couldn't be right; a striker who has been in the game for 10 years and played for England must have averaged more than 5 a season. Minutes later, Vassell ran clean through after a short Davis backpass...and slid it wide. A further few minutes later, a stunning Petrov cross found Vassell's feet in the six yard box...he controlled it, hesitated, then got mugged by Big Dave. If it had just hit his knee in the first place it was a goal. My revised opinion was "How the hell has he scored nearly 50 goals?"

February 2008

Premier League Table 1ˢᵗ February 2008

		P	W	D	L	Pts	GD
17	Birmingham	24	5	5	14	20	-13
18	Wigan	24	5	5	14	20	-17
19	Fulham	24	2	10	12	16	-19
20	Derby	24	1	5	18	8	-39

Results:

02.02.08 Birmingham 1-1 Derby County

09.02.08 Derby County 0-3 Spurs

23.02.08 Wigan 2-0 Derby County

Following on from the draw against Man City, a point at Birmingham left the Rams on the cusp of three matches unbeaten - with the erratic Tottenham at home to follow. Just like every other home game where we thought we had a chance, the Rams folded without a whimper and lost 0-3.

The Birmingham match though, was a rare treat. The game itself, quality wise, was absolutely dreadful, although we were the visitors so it's excusable to some degree. The difference with the point at Birmingham was that it was slightly unexpected. Thus far, most Rams points had come from matches where we had left a bit disappointed that we hadn't won (e.g. Bolton, Fulham and even Man City). At Birmingham, the Rams were losing 0-1 with the game petering out. Then in the final moments, substitute Tito Villa headed home a cross in front of the travelling Rams fans and a point was surprisingly and ecstatically won . The walk out of the stadium was hairy to say the least. The Birmingham chairman had billed it a "must win" game before the kick-off which seemed a ludicrous exaggeration at the time. However, failure to beat the worst Premier League team ever was ultimately to cost Birmingham their Premier League status.

As earlier mentioned, the Spurs game was a huge letdown followed by an equally big disappointment at Wigan, regarded by Rams fans, Jewell and neutrals as one of the worst top flight spectacles ever.

The jury was still out in regards to the new signings. Robert barely lasted the first month before being seen as a gamble that hadn't worked. Bar Villa's goal at St. Andrews, he and Sterjovski weren't convincing, Ghaly was undoubtedly talented but had yet to have the desired impact. The biggest surprise of all was that Robbie Savage didn't appear to be the real Robbie Savage. The minimum we expected was a figure head to gee the team up and get in peoples faces. So far Savage had politely run around bothering neither players nor fans.

One small footnote at the end of the month was Michael Johnson joining Notts County on loan for the rest of the season. Jonno was not part of the plans after promotion and joined Sheffield Wednesday on loan. He rejoined the Rams around Christmas and played four games, including the Liverpool match and didn't look particularly better or worse than his team mates. Simon went to see Notts County in an end of season match as the Magpies fought to stay in the league. Again, Jonno looked neither better nor worse than his team mates, which tells you something about the quality of the Rams squad.

February 3rd

With our dire form this season, it's often been difficult to find an angle for the Times column or the Observer phone call. When Birmingham took the field to Steps' "Tragedy" I immediately clocked it was a great pun waiting to happen, all it needed now was for the Blues to suffer a tragedy.

I know some Rams fans weren't keen on Robbie Savage's arrival but I'm sure even the biggest sceptics would enjoy his latest wind up. Apparently before the match, he claimed to have been Birmingham's best player *ever*. The chap from the Observer told me this but I took it to mean whilst Savage was there. I replied "well they got relegated when he left so he probably was". I realised he meant "ever" when the Birmingham fan in the paper started going on about Trevor Francis.

To add further salt to the wound, how about this from Jewell in the press conference, when asked about Derby's equaliser:
Q: "So what can you tell us about Villa?"
Jewell: "Well, I think they're the top team in Birmingham, aren't they?"
Who'd have thought a scrappy draw against Birmingham would give us so much pleasure?

Article written for the Times Fanzone after the 1-1 draw against Birmingham
Derby joy is Blues Tragedy
In this modern age when sports psychologists are part of the furniture and "positive thinking" is more advice-down-the-pub than psychobabble, should a team who take the field to "Tragedy" really feel aggrieved at conceding a last minute equaliser? (Alternatively, "should a team who take the field to Steps etc..."). As Birmingham's self-fulfilling prophecy came true, it was Derby fans who had a rare occasion to dance.

The fact that Derby should be so overjoyed with a point against Birmingham tells you all you need to know about the Rams' season. Both teams were promoted last year and with all due respect to the Blues (who have won points at Anfield and Emirates; our record for the corresponding fixtures is P2 L2 GD -11) we wouldn't have anticipated a draw at St. Andrews would be one of the highlights of the season.

The game itself was almost completely bereft of quality. One of today's papers tried to put the blame firmly at Derby's door (Derby "...don't half drag teams down") but in fairness we went with an attacking 4-2-4 and the fact that we couldn't get or keep the ball was no excuse for Birmingham's failure to be better.

However, as a Rams fan, the last few minutes showed the true magic of football. Even in the darkest corner of the darkest season, you can have a moment where - for a spilt second - you feel like you've won the World Cup. Villa's in-off-the-post in-front-of-the-away-fans equaliser was one of those. If you're a dyed in the wool fan of anyone you'll know exactly what I mean. If you're not - you won't and will probably never understand.

February 4th

Apparently Bywater was 2 or 3 weeks away from fitness last week and didn't even make the bench against Man City. This Saturday he played a full game for Ipswich. Presumably not part of Jagger's plans then.

February 5th

The latest example of football gone mad: a lad at work told me today how after the rigorous body search of away fans at Birmingham he was told "you can't take that in with you". He had his Kit-Kat confiscated. What damage could you possibly do with a Kit-Kat? To my reckoning, with the traditional 4-finger style, you could just about reach the home fans by using an underarm skimming technique. Even then the only person at risk would be a passing diabetic succumbing to temptation. With the chunky version, I suppose you could punch someone in the face whilst gripping one.

The only chocolate bars you could possibly do any harm with in terms of a) being able to launch it a fair distance and b) coming keen if it hit you on the temple are the king sized Mars or Yorkie - ironically the only two chocolate bars you will see for sale in a football ground! (Birmingham City also offer a selection of hot drinks for pouring on away fans from the upper tier).

February 6th

From an article about gay athletes in the Observer Sport Monthly:
"False rumours that Graeme Le Saux was gay started in his own dressing room, when his team mates discovered he had spent his holiday with defender Ken Monkou. "All of a sudden everyone was making jokes about "camping with Ken","Le Saux has said. In his autobiography, *Left Field,* Le Saux describes the abuse. "I got plenty of comments from other players about being a faggot or a queer, Robbie Savage seemed to get a particular thrill out of it"."

I wonder why those Chelsea pranksters (probably Vinny Jones, Dennis Wise et al during that time) chose to target Le Saux rather than giant Central Defender Ken Monkou? A misdirected comment towards Monkou could have saved us a whole decade of Dennis Wise. For those who don't remember Ken Monkou, he's 6' 3" tall and almost as wide.

Meanwhile, the debate rumbles on about the most dangerous chocolate bar with the suggestion that a Snickers Duo could be used as a pair of nunchackers.

February 9th

(written on the morning of the Tottenham match)

Today's game looks like being a sell-out. A Tottenham fan at work was planning to go and I asked him the other day if he had his ticket yet (at this point there were a couple of hundred left). He said he hadn't as Derby weren't activating any new customer numbers because of the number of Spurs fans trying to register and buy tickets. Whilst listening, I was thinking to myself "at the end of this conversation I'll make a truly kind gesture that will warm the cockles of his heart - I'll offer my customer number". He finished by saying "...we thought 'fair enough', we wouldn't be happy if away fans were buying tickets at White Hart Lane and taking Spurs fans tickets". I thought "good point, well made", nodded and strolled off.

February 10th

When announcing the attendance for yesterday's game, the chap on the tannoy added the usual "Derby County would like to thank you for your continued loyal support". So what thanks do we get for continuing to buy tickets despite the absolutely dreadful home form? Prices up by a tenner (30% if you prefer) for our next home game - which is incidentally one of the least attractive of the season *(Sunderland at home)*. We love you too.

As the Spurs game approached a sell-out, I wonder what the thoughts were amongst the clubs bean-counters: "Great, what wonderful, loyal fans we have" or "shit, we could have charged them more for that one"?

February 11th

In the aftermath of Man U. getting doubled by City at the weekend, Carlos Queiroz had a moan about players being tired from international duty in the week. A few weeks ago United had a rare week with no internationals, no Champions League and no domestic league or Cup. So how did they use these valuable few days? They flew the first team squad to the Middle East and back to play a friendly in the desert climate of Saudi Arabia. (Allegedly paid a million quid - claims of "it's not about the money" were especially thin on this one). I'm sure your players *are* feeling jaded Carlos.

Ferguson defended the trip by saying "We have gone away before in mid-season and it has worked well for us. We went to Dubai a couple of years ago and we won the FA Cup at the end of that season". If we had won the cup, great, let's go every year. But Man U? Wouldn't it be more accurate to say "We went to Dubai a couple of years ago and didn't win the league"?

February 12th

Whilst searching for something on Bob Malcolm, Chris stumbled across an FC Dallas website where people where discussing a rumour that he was joining them. Here are some excerpts:

So, what do we know about the Bobster?

– He's a center back / holding mid.

– He played 88 times for Rangers before being released.

– He's probably banned from English football for somewhere between 15-20 months due to his recent drunk driving incident....

Wow. "Sleepy" Bob Malcolm a member of FC Dallas? Will he join us at Lochrann's for a pint? Wax poetic about the Old Firm games he was a part of? Maybe he'd even drive us home after the games...

Nothing on this end of the pond seems to have suggested him, so the Brit media is likely behind the times (like the rest of that country)*.

Why MLS? Well his options in the UK appear to be limited now. Additionally he is the kind of colorful 'tasty character' which some believe MLS needs more of to add personality and controversy to the league, thus generating 'water-cooler' discussion.

*I know the US like to see themselves as the world authority on most things but world leaders on Bob Malcolm speculation is pushing it a bit.

February 13th

I was in a rush yesterday so a few further comments on yesterdays Bob Malcolm story:

"the Bobster": what a great nickname. I think Earnie should re-invent himself as "the Bobster" next year and forget this season ever happened. Being banned from driving and being banned from football are not the same thing (ask Vincent Pericard - although being incarcerated can restrict your appearances).

I fear for the future of the MLS if Bob Malcolm is the kind of character to "add personality" to the league. Or maybe we are behind the times? (as the other bloke suggested). Are our silly notions of skill and talent just Saxon helmet (i.e. old hat)?

February 14th

Can you imagine a team with a worse record than ours? A team without a win all season, a team whose last 4 games include defeats of 0-5, 0-6 and 0-8 conceding an average of 3.4 goals a game. Allow me to introduce...Derby County reserves.

In fairness, we've fielded a team of kids in most games but on Tuesday night against Reading we had a first team squad midfield and attack of Feilhaber, Jones, Teale, Lewis, Earnshaw and Sterjovski - and still got hammered 5-0.

February 16th

We had an unprecedented amount of activity in the Ramspace post box last week with two emails in as many days (usually we're lucky to get one a month between us - and you call *us* lazy bastards!?).

One was about the Premier League's plan to play games abroad and the offer to colonise world football being met with a collective "you're all right thanks mate" from the FAs of the world. There's a lot you could say about the whole fiasco so I won't even start but thought I'd share a story: It was suggested that Bangalore could be one of the venues, in fairness, by one of the newspapers rather than the FA. I go to Bangalore every year and a couple of years ago went to watch a Test match - India v. Australia. A major sporting fixture by any standards.

The seats in our area were simple white garden chairs with numbers written on them. As people began to arrive and recognise their mates, they simply took their seat with them and swapped chairs, so they stayed in the correct seat number but for example, seat B25 was now situated between P92 and P94. One bright spark decided he would like a bit more leg and elbow room - so took his seat to sit in the middle of the gangway. He was soon joined by many others until going anywhere was an obstacle course. As the sun rose, others went for a walkabout to sit in the shade. In another area of the ground, people in the cheap standing area were slipping a few rupees through the fence and being passed a chair from the more pricey seating area. Soon the standing and seating areas were reversed. As for the food and drink - that was a man-tangle of epic proportions.

Let's hope the Premier League send their finest stewards along - I'd love to see some of those little Hitlers try and sort that out!

February 18th

The other email, as mentioned in the last entry, referred to the Departure Lounge article with a comment along the lines of "I'll be interested to see what you come up with for Benny Feilhaber's best moment when he inevitably leaves in the summer".

Heads are being scratched as we speak.

February 19th

Simon suggested that Feilhaber's finest moment at the club could have been the opening of Starbucks. I remember that he was due to open it alongside Lewis but I only saw Lewis in the ensuing publicity photographs. Could this have been a strange microcosm of Benny Fill's Rams career? Earmarked as having all the skills and attributes to do the job but ultimately he just didn't get the call.

February 21st

It's been a strange few weeks for Celtic midfielder Barry Robson. On the eve of the transfer deadline, Dundee Utd. accepted a million pound bid for him from lower division also-rans Nottingham Forest (you may have heard of them, we played them a few years ago). Celtic then matched the offer and Baz, not surprisingly, decided to join Celtic.

Had he signed for Forest, he would have spent Tuesday travelling up to Carlisle - only for the lower division scrap to be postponed due to bad weather. As it was, on Wednesday he played and scored in front of 60,000 fans at Celtic Park against Barcelona.

Next week he'll probably be playing in the Nou Camp. Forest's next away match is Leyton Orient.

February 23rd

The first signs of American Sports Marketing can now be seen - A family ticket for the Sunderland game includes 2 Adult tickets, 2 Junior tickets, 4 Coca-Colas and 4 Hot Dogs (and a mini ball for some reason).

No doubt half time entertainment will soon be on the agenda. English football has many quirks, so for the benefit of any new board members here's one of them: although football crowds are mostly male, there is very little interest in watching scantily dressed cheerleaders. What would be far preferable is to get some slightly overweight fans in normal shoes and jeans to take penno's against the Youth team 'keeper (I can even supply you with some contestants if you want). That's a few hundred quid on a focus group saved.

February 24th

A unanimous verdict on yesterday's game at Wigan. My brother did The Verdict for the Observer and the paragraph included: "If there was a worse match in all four divisions I'm glad I didn't see it... [I can't] think of a worse Derby display in the last 10 years". The main report included the line "...a sure-fire contender for the worst Premier League game of the season". Paul Jewell called it "...the worst performance I've ever, ever seen from a so-called Premier League team". The victorious Wigan fan in The Verdict summarised "It was awful".

On a lighter note...

By pure coincidence following yesterdays entry, I got a text from my brother about half time penalty shoot-outs (he was en route to Wigan via Blackpool so wouldn't have read the entry). It read "half time penno shoot out music is Beta Band! Think its Smile off 1st LP".

The track in question is obscure to say the least; an album track from an album 10 years old. The song itself is a ten minute long near instrumental with a sporadic singing gnome refrain. The record buying public voted with their feet on that one; the commercial splash made was similar to that of Rams shirts emblazoned with "3 Griffin".

So now we have the dream ticket - fat blokes, slippy shoes, singing gnomes. To coin a phrase - what's not to like?

(If this all sounds a bit surreal, remember how many times we've seen penalty shoot outs between two grown men in animal costumes. An unsuspecting away mascot in inflatable It's A Knockout boots against Rammie in his Adidas Predators).

February 25th

The Observer often throw some random statistics into their results service and this week they had a Premier League "Aerial duels won" list. Remarkably, Steve Howard was sixth, despite not playing in the Premier League for two months and not always being a regular when he did (the count is actual duels won rather than a percentage).

Stats can be twisted to prove anything but here are a few things this may tell us:

1) We played an awful lot of long balls when Howard was here.

2) We really should have had someone up front with him at all times as it seems he was doing "his job" quite well.

3) A couple of decent wingers would have made things interesting.

4) It's a shame some of them didn't end up in the net.

(To correct myself on yesterdays entry before some other smart Alec does - the Beta Band track in question is actually called "Smiling", has far more vocals than I remember and is a mere eight and a half minutes long).

February 26th

Evidently a quiet day for football news, the Derby Telegraph reported a story from Psychic News (Psycho News might be more accurate reading this one) about a "dog that celebrated promotion" in May last year. The story claims "throughout that season, one or two people had reported an unusual black dog hanging around outside the ground". Before you call Ghostbusters - I've got a black dog and often coupled walkies with a trip to the ticket office (when it was outside). Presumably talking about the celebrations, the story then reads "Some say they saw it...jumping around

excitedly and doing somersaults". I think half of Derby was seeing
somersaulting dogs by the end of Promotion night!

February 27th

A few seasons ago when the Rams played Stoke away, Ade Akinbiyi
"scored" and ran off to the corner flag to celebrate, closely followed by
several amorous Stoke players. However, the linesman had flagged and the
goal was disallowed. Derby took a quick free-kick and ran almost
unopposed to the other end where Adam Bolder (from memory) put the
ball in the Stoke net. The ref then disallowed our "goal" for reasons unclear
in the away end. He said afterwards that the free kick was either from the
wrong place or didn't properly leave the area - some bullshit. Stoke scored in
injury time and we lost 1-0.

(you're probably now thinking "I know all that, what's your point?")

Last weekend in the Real Madrid v. Getafe match, an almost identical
situation occurred... but this time the ref didn't bottle it. It was the only goal
of the game and Getafe won 1-0.

February 28th

I'm reading Stan Ternent's book at the moment "Stan the Man". There's
that much material in there that I'll probably write a full article for the main
zine. However, this anecdote just can't wait:

(Stan's team Bury are losing 1-0 at Bradford and a 20-man brawl has
erupted)

"Months of frustration were being exorcised by a good old scrap. From
nowhere Paul Jewell, who was assistant manager to Chris Kamara at
Bradford, appeared and got stuck in.

No one touches my players. I wasn't having it...I dragged him into the dugout, dug him in the ribs and bashed his head against the roof. Suddenly he didn't want to get stuck in any more".

I'm sure they are best of pals by the last chapter.

March 2008

Premier League Table 1ˢᵗ March 2008

		P	W	D	L	Pts	GD
17	Birmingham	27	5	8	14	23	-13
18	Reading	27	6	4	17	22	-24
19	Fulham	27	3	10	14	19	-20
20	Derby	27	1	6	20	9	-44

Results:

01.03.08 Derby County 0-0 Sunderland

12.03.08 Chelsea 6-1 Derby County

15.03.08 Derby County 0-1 Man United

22.03.08 Middlesbrough 1-0 Derby County

29.03.08 Derby County 2-2 Fulham

March was the month when the Rams were officially relegated. The first team ever in Premier League history to be relegated in March. The month contained home matches against two other relegation candidates - Fulham and Sunderland, and Derby earned two draws from the two fixtures. Our revised target was avoiding the lowest points ever record so the two points gained were welcome but the games were also our best chance of bagging all three against anyone. We went from one extreme to the other against Chelsea and Man United (hammered by Chelsea, unlucky to lose against Man Utd.) before, yet again, a weak performance against Middlesbrough when the game was up for grabs.

We were none the wiser about the new signings; Stubbs got injured after initially adding some quality; Savage had a false dawn with an outstanding performance against Man United; and Ghlay came back from being dropped to star in the defeat at Middlesbrough. Villa became joint top scorer with a brace against Fulham, although one of the goals hit him whilst he was facing the other way - not a great endorsement of his awareness around the box.

The "exit" door continued to revolve with several players joining Championship teams on loan. Gary Teale had already joined Plymouth and was joined in the second tier by Craig Fagan signing for Hull and Stephen Pearson joining Stoke at the last minute. The latter two players were both with a view to a permanent summer move and involved hefty loan fees (rumoured to be £500,000 in Pearson's case. He started just three games for the Potters and returned to the Rams in the summer). Derby had no chance of surviving so Jewell, quite rightly, added to next year's budget.

Off the field, the big story was a "sex scandal" involving Paul Jewell. The News Of The World had unearthed an old tape of Jewell cavorting with a women who wasn't his wife and made the story front page news. Given Jewell's appalling record thus far as Rams manager, there was some speculation that this might be an ideal excuse to get rid of him. However, the story died a death very quickly with little comment from either Jewell or the club.

The Journals of Derventio – March

March 2nd

(Written after the 0-0 draw with Sunderland)

There were quite a few things about yesterday's game that made me realise how low expectations had fallen nowadays. When Sterjovski was subbed I said something like "he was alright" which was immediately contested by the Jackal. When I considered for a moment I thought - he played right wing yet didn't take on or beat his man once, he didn't put any decent crosses in and he hasn't had a shot. I suppose what I had meant is that he hadn't made any catastrophic errors - and that's about all we can ask nowadays. Similarly, when Villa was subbed, quite a few people gave him a standing ovation. The fact is, he'd done absolutely nothing. Sunderland were also dreadful but I think everyone, myself included, was overjoyed just to be getting a point. They even played "Chelsea Dagger" at the final whistle, a song usually reserved for celebrations like lifting the play-off trophy or drawing at home to Bolton.

There was more of the same in this mornings Observer, where the Rams fan in The Verdict gave Kenny Miller a 9/10 making him centre-forward in Team of The Week. Miller wasn't bad but again - surely we should expect more than two speculative efforts against a defence with a worse away record than ours? (The same bloke also awarded Roy Carroll a "4" for keeping an ultra rare Rams clean sheet - this bizarrely made him the 'keeper in the Flops of the Week team.)

March 3rd

I wrote last week about how stats can be used to prove one thing or another. This weeks Observer printed a table entitled "Couldn't Hit A Cow's..." showing players with the most shots off target. The top three were

Adebayor, Ronaldo and Torres. The Premier League's top scorers are also Ronaldo, Adebayor and Torres. I think a better title would have been "If you don't shoot, you don't score". (The Rams of course have very few shots off target).

Another set of stats showed players with the lowest Tackle Success Rate with our own Dean Leacock featured in the bottom five. Not to worry though, he was joined by Carragher and Jenas whilst the Top 5 feature such hard men as Seb Larsson, Julio Arca and Mikel Arteta. It all begs the question - Does someone actually get paid for compiling all this?

March 4th

I see the reserves lost again last night. One thing Jewell and Davies seem to be in agreement over is the policy of not playing senior players. A few have played once or twice but in the main it's been a team of kids. There must be some thinking behind this (avoiding injuries probably) but I reckon there's a few "pros" to outweigh the "cons": the chance for Earnie to get a few semi-competitive goals; Robert to get his match fitness up; or Feilhaber and Villa to get acclimatised. The younger players also benefit from playing alongside experienced pro's and not getting battered by grown men every week.

I think I'm on safe ground to offer an opinion here: both teams are rock bottom; the first team is (and has all season been) full of players low in sharpness and confidence; no young players have earned a call-up despite our ongoing desperation for anyone or anything to improve the side. I can't see anyone turning round and saying "it's working fine".

March 5th

We have a scheme at work where if you have a company mobile you can pay £10 a month and use it for personal calls. If you go significantly over - you pay the difference. Fair enough. In January, as you may have read, I had a couple of trips away and the wife was also abroad visiting family. I expected a bigger phone bill and duly received one - I was about £9 over, better than I'd expected.

However, when I looked at the bill, the cost of my international calls, texts and even receiving calls abroad was minimal. "Where's this going?" you may be wondering. Well, on the day I decided to go to the Birmingham match, I must have rung the ticket office at least 10 times (sounds a lot but a few consecutive tries in the morning, the same at lunch and the same in the afternoon). I didn't succeed in speaking to anyone, just heard the same long recorded message about office opening hours, menu options etc. before being told no-one was available. Sometimes I held for a couple of minutes, sometimes not at all. When I looked at my bill, this had cost me over eight quid! So don't stay on hold if you're phoning for tickets. I think it's 25p a minute; criminal for someone in Derby phoning somewhere else in Derby - a stealth tax if ever there was one. The ironic thing was, I subsequently found out that Birmingham tickets were only available in-person from the ground.

March 6th

A Hull Fan At Work was telling me today how referee Mike Riley had ruined the Hull v. Burnley match on Tuesday by losing control and sending off two players from each side. The second Burnley player in a Poll-esque farce where he booked him for something innocuous but was then reminded he'd have to send him off. It wasn't sour grapes, Hull won 2-0. As the conversation continued it made me realise quite how much Riley had contributed to our dire spectacle on Saturday (although the Jackal will remind me that he pointed this out several times during the match). When I checked the paper, it showed that Riley had blown up for an astonishing 40 fouls in what could never be described as a dirty game (evenly spread 21/19) add to this offsides, goal kicks, corners, throw-ins and substitutions and you're talking a lot of breaks in play. With each one taking time, it's little wonder no one had time to score. Obviously with a decent ref we'd have been able to play our free flowing Total Football of choice and won handsomely. If in doubt blame the ref.

I'm off for the weekend, see you next week.

March 10th

Arriving home from a place with intermittent mobile signal, it was only today that I properly found out about Craig Fagan's departure. There's more to be said on this one but I'll save it for another day as there's too much to do around the house. But I'll leave this thought with you: Craig Fagan is/was the Premier League's worst winger.

I've quoted stats from the Observer for the last couple of weeks and realise its lazy and possibly bordering on copyright infringement to continue - but just one more...

Craig Fagan crossed the ball 67 times this season with a 6% success rate. To put it another way - he crossed the ball 67 times this season and played a "decent" ball 4 times - the worst ratio in the Premier League. We weren't all mistaken, he was rubbish. I also read that, along with Pearo, he played more games than anyone, so this wasn't a freak statistic based on a couple of games. As I said, more to come on this one.

March 11th

I was talking to the oft quoted Hull fan last Thursday about the Tigers promotion campaign when he jokingly, if not mockingly, asked "I don't suppose you have any striker-cum-right-wingers who are surplus to requirements?". This chap usually tells me who Hull are signing several weeks in advance but had no inkling of this one. He then gave me a quick resume of Fagan's Hull career:

Fagan was signed by Hull as a centre forward from Colchester for £125,000. He tended to pull wide a lot and not score so the then Hull manager Peter Taylor decided to play him on the wing. Fagan had a strop, fell out with Taylor and fell out the picture. After Taylor's departure, Fagan reappeared. It was the last year of Fagan's contract, he found a bit of form and scored a few goals (bumped up by penalty taking duties). Opinions amongst Hull fans ranged from "we could get our money back" to "if someone offers £350,000 we'll bite their hand off". When the Rams paid £750,000, there was a collective jaw dropping around the city of Hull (the Hull fan has previously said that we also paid a £250k bonus on gaining promotion. Not mentioned down here but common knowledge in Hull apparently).

I'm seeing the Hull fan at a conference tomorrow. It would be nice to greet him from afar with a loud Craig Fagan chant. The problem is that even after a year at the club - there isn't one. I think that sums up Fagan's Rams career as much as anything.

There were a few emails on the subject at work today. A couple of us picked up on Phil Brown's comment about Fagan having experience in "getting over the finishing line". I pointed out that we were top when he signed and finished third, no thanks to his contribution. A bloke replied "I suppose you could say he was our Tino Asprilla - but without the skill, goals, back-flips and guns".

(In the interests of fairness, Davies did Fagan no favours by repeated playing him on the left wing. No doubt he'll bag a hatful for Hull).*

*I needn't have bothered covering my back, Fagan failed to score for Hull in their promotion run-in.

March 12th

I saw the Hull fan today, apparently Fagan got quite a warm welcome on Saturday and they are generally pleased to see him back.

I'm listening to the Chelsea match on Radio Derby at the moment but I don't know if I'll make it until the end. Not because of the Rams but Ross Fletcher's sudden love affair with Chelsea. Until forty odd minutes, the talk was all about how well Derby were equipping themselves. Only twenty minutes later, Ross is not only purring over (Derby have gone from 0-3 to 0-5 during this paragraph!), well by now purring over everything. We've had him eulogising not only about Chelsea's attack but also Terry, Carvalho and even the Chelsea stadium!

The score's getting worse and I haven't heard Ross this excited since the Play-Off semi...

March 13th

I wasn't the only one irritated by Ross Fletcher's star-struck commentary of last night's game between Chelsea and some team at the bottom of the league whose name escapes me.

Simon also picked up on Fletcher's discussion with Colin Gibson near the start about parts of Stamford Bridge being in need of renovation, only for it to be transformed into a "wonderful stadium" as the goals rolled in. The same applied to the fans - during the first half there was apparently no atmosphere and the fans were quiet but later on Fletcher gleefully announced "Chelsea fans are loving this!". Is it too much too ask for a Derby commentator to be partial? Surely some "sing when you're winning comments" would have been more apt. I would also have mentioned the Stan The Man [Stan Ternent's autobiography] fact regarding Chelsea pulling in only 7,000 at The Bridge barely a decade ago. In fact I would have mentioned this a few times building up to a "where were you when you were shit!" crescendo at 5 or 6 nil.

The other point that bugged me, mentioned briefly yesterday but again for emphasis, was as follows: at half time the summary was basically that we had competed well but conceded a soft penalty and gifted them a second moments before half time. About ten minutes into the second half Fletcher said something like "I was saying to someone at half time how you have to see Chelsea in the flesh to realise how good they are etc. etc..." (must have been off air Ross) followed by an unending flow about their class. No mention of "yes, you're all queuing up for the 5th and 6th but where were you on Saturday when the going got tough?" *[Chelsea had just been knocked out of the F.A. Cup at Barnsley...]* or "Six goals against bottom of the league is big of you but little consolation for getting dumped from two cups in little over a week is it?" *[...and also lost the Carling Cup Final against Spurs]*. You may have guessed, I'm not especially keen on Chelsea.

March 15th

If you wanted a clue about Jewell's plans for the team next season - look no further than the "We Are Derby" season ticket advertising on the official website. It is dominated by Jewell signings with many regulars passed over for the inclusion of bit part players Villa and Sterjovski (although the latter is now nailed on for right wing without Teale, Fagan and Barnes). Stubbs and Savage also feature with Jay McEveley the sole remnant from the Davies era (it's a fair bet Jay is "part of the plans" as he's featured a lot under Jagger). To be properly representative of the City in line with the "We Are Derby" slogan (and to avoid looking like an Everton team group from the 80's), there are, quite rightly, a couple of black lads in the picture. Neither is instantly recognisable and they bear the squad numbers 50 and 52. This is not boding well for Moore, Davis, Jonno, Fagan or Earnie. (Although in

Jonno and Fagan's case, being loaned out from a wafer thin squad is probably the bigger hint).

March 17th

The makeover of all things Derby County continues apace with the introduction of Darude's techno banger "Sandstorm" now accompanying the teams onto the field. At several hundred b.p.m.'s faster than "Steve Bloomer's Watching", it was long overdue and should induce some excitement in the crowd. Many a time we've seen a ref waiting to kick off whilst the funeral march of "Bloomer" reaches its crescendo. At least now if Sandstorm overruns, the ref can have a boogie and blow his whistle in an acid house style-ee.

I had a couple of texts from Simon on the subject. The first on Saturday afternoon moments after the tune had played at top volume to 33,000 excited souls "...I was loving it. Clapping along like a maniac..." The second on Monday afternoon from a quiet office near Long Eaton "Playing Darude Sandstorm on Radio one. I'm clapping like a lunatic". I hope some CCTV footage exists of the latter.

March 18th

The latest immigration scandal...

Last August, talking about Benny Feilhaber at a Work Permit appeal, the USA national coach told the Home Office "Feilhaber was now an automatic selection and one of the best midfielders produced by the USA in recent years". Last week, Feilhaber failed to make the final cut for a USA under 23 pre-Olympic squad. Someone phone the Daily Mail quick! (I dread to think of the yarn spun to get Claude Davis his stamp during his appeal around the same time).

March 19th

A couple of random statistics about attendances:

I had a few digs at Leeds last season about dwindling crowds but gave them some begrudging praise earlier this season for getting 30,000 a few times in League 1. Well, I take it back. Now they've stopped winning, 1 in 3 isn't bothering to turn up anymore and they're back down to circa 20,000 (still impressive as such but not by absent 10,000. Never mind, I'm sure they'll be back for the play-offs, probably moaning about lack of tickets).*
Secondly: Wigan played Derby and Arsenal at home within the space of three weeks. The Derby match pulled a bigger crowd. Why? I don't know. Arsenal took at least as many fans as us (as it looked on the TV) so it was purely down to home fans. Perhaps my philosophy of "I pay to see us win, not watch the opposition" is popular up there.

This was true when Leeds reached the Play-Off final versus Doncaster. Doncaster had to suspend the sale of tickets because of Leeds fans purchasing extras.

March 21st

It was only a couple of days ago when looking for something else, that I read Jewell's comments on the Fagan deal. From what I'd heard, the Fagan deal was loan to permanent with a fee agreed for the summer. However, according to Jewell: "He wants to play up-front and there is an opportunity at Hull for him to do that...that doesn't mean Craig Fagan is out of the picture here for next season, it just means he wants to play for Hull at the moment".

Whatever next, Stephen Pearson joins Stenhousemuir on loan because they want him to play in goal and he's up for it?

It seems that Fagan's delusion that he is a centre forward continues despite failing to even outscore mostly absent defender Lewin Nyatanga for two seasons running. Ironically, he will probably be further down the pecking order at Hull than with ul with Campbell, Folan and Windass all in front. Maybe he'll get a game on the wing?

(Fago's story so far at Hull: Makes his debut whilst Folan is suspended and Windass injured. Fagan himself gets injured in his second game. Hull proceed to win 5-0 and 1-3 in the following matches with Folan and Windass back and firing on all cylinders).

March 21st (part2)

I've just had a quick read of some recent Rams Trust articles on the Telegraph website (an apt subtitle would be "woe, woe and thrice woe"). One paragraph particularly caught my eye:

"A major factor [in the takeover] was the club's fan base, which he [Tom Glick] described as "off the hook". Translating to our English understanding of this phrase, this American marketing jargon might read 'off the peg', or 'ready made.'"

If that was the case I would also add "taken for granted" and be quite annoyed by it.

However, courtesy of several R n' B songs on Radio 1 (and a CSS album track) I know that "off the hook" means something quite different. According to the Urban Dictionary "Cool, awesome, crazy, amazing, hot, fly, wicked, awesome, rad, the shit, badass", all which translates as "rather good old bean!".

We could be in for a rocky ride with the traditionalists.

March 23rd

If you haven't seen the Paul Jewell story yet, click on the link below, it contains some of the best puns ever:

[This refers to a News Of The World front page featuring a Paul Jewell sex tape which was allegedly two or three years old. The story contained several references to "ramming", "scoring", "failing to score", "extra time" etc. etc.]

Thanks to the reader who sent me the link.

At the time of writing, I don't know what the outcome of this one will be. I can't imagine GSE will be impressed in the slightest given their family oriented marketing approach (family ticket offers, family Easter egg hunts at Pride Park, Glick's regular mention of his family including the puppies). I've got no anti-Jewell sentiments at all but given a moment's consideration, what could you say in his favour? Most people would say "he seems a decent, honest bloke" but that doesn't seem the best description of him all of a sudden.

There are echoes of the Bob Malcolm situation as well. It's a non-footballing matter and if it was [insert name of good or valuable player here. I can't think of one] it would probably be brushed under the carpet. However, if some of the unknown investors are getting twitchy about Jewell's winless streak - now could be the ideal opportunity. I don't think there'd be many fans wielding placards either - yes, Jewell had an impossible task, and yes, we've had a stack of injuries but judging on results only - could it have been any worse?

Several weeks ago (or was it months?) Simon prophetically said "this could be another Gregory situation" as the Rams continued to lose (he also said this at Boro yesterday). Optimism + expectation + bad results + worse results. You can now add "+ sleaze"* to the equation as the parallels increase.

A recurring theme in Stan Ternent's book is his desire to manage in the Premiership. What's the odds on "it's not in the circumstances I would have wanted...but Paul's given me his blessing...it's only for seven games but if it goes well who knows?". It didn't do Phil Brown any harm at Hull.

*For legal purposes - accusations of misconduct against Gregory were unproven and the charges dropped.

March 24th

The Daily Star picked up the baton today with the headline "Prem Boss Stars in Net Porn". I didn't buy it but from I could gather it was a non-story speculating about the possibility of Jewell's video ending up on the net. It suggests that "portly Paul" could be the Premier League's Paris Hilton by suggesting "the footage could turn him into an unlikely internet sex star like heiress Paris, 27."

Really? Could Jewell be releasing sub-standard pop singles in a couple of years? I can't imagine Jewell holding quite the same attraction myself but The Star assures us "...there is a massive market in freaky tapes...". Ouch! Being an outsider to the mysterious world of football, I just can't imagine how players react to this kind of thing. Will Jewell's credibility and authority be undermined by the whole thing? Or will he be greeted with shouts of "Hurrraahhh!!! Get in there Gaffer!" followed by High Fives and Big Tens up and down Moor Farm?

(I fully expect the Journals to rocket up the search engines with the mention of "porn", "sex" and "Paris Hilton" in the space of a couple of paragraphs.)

March 25th

After Sunday's excitement, the Jewell story now seems to be yesterday's chip papers, with a few words in the news section of the Derby Telegraph stating that the video wouldn't affect Jewell's position at the club, according to Adam Pearson. Never one to court controversy, Steve Nicholson uses his column to criticise the behaviour and conduct of Chelsea players, worrying about the bad example being set to kids. Best not to mention Shaggers antics.

No crimes have been committed though and it didn't do Sven any harm. So now on to the weekend's other scandal - the performance at Middlesbrough. The first half was one of the worst I've ever seen. Many of the after match quotes spoke of a much improved second half. Yes, with an arctic wind behind us we had more of the ball and Ghaly looked quality but even with three strikers on the field, Schwarzer didn't have one save to make.

A word on Middlesbrough: it's fair to say they haven't got the greatest image. Hated by some, disliked by others and worst of all - their local "rivals" are completely indifferent to them. My opinion of them recently rose after reading in the fact rich Stan The Man, that Boro had the highest crowds in the country per head of population (this would have been around 2002). To be fair, the place isn't even a City and has a significantly smaller population than Derby so some of the stick they endure about empty seats is a bit harsh.

We spoke to some Boro fans before the match in the drinker and the chippy; they knew exactly the situation they were in. For saying Boro are one of the few English teams to get anywhere in Europe recently, there was no inflated expectation. One bloke told me he'd be quite happy being sixth in the Championship and winning most weeks rather than scratting around in the Prem. I don't know whether he was trying to make me feel better about next season but he certainly succeeded!

March 26th

Spare a thought for poor Gretna. Their recent financial woes have been well publicised - unpaid players, calling in the Administrators and uncertainty whether the club will even finish the season. After a few harsh weeks, a lot was riding on a bumper crowd against Celtic to ensure survival for another few weeks. However, after problems with the Fir Park pitch (Gretna's temporary home just outside Glasgow), the game was switched to Livingston's ground with no cash sales on the day. As a result just 3,651 attended, surely one of the lowest crowds ever for a match involving Celtic. Baffled by footballs inflexible bureaucracy, the Gretna manager lamented: "I don't know if I'm just a silly old sod but where is the common sense? If there is a pay-gate on the day, what are they expecting, the Khmer Rouge with Kalashnikovs or football supporters?" A very good point. You can't be too liberal though, next thing you know you'll have people trying to smuggle in Kit-Kats. (If this is lost on you - a lad a work had a Kit-Kat confiscated after a rigorous body search at Birmingham away as documented in the Journals early Feb).

March 27th

The Jackal has just laid his hands on a couple of freebies for the Fulham game. I was planning to get a refund for the ones we already had but he advised "...or swap them for Villa...just make sure they don't give you Tito!"

March 28th

One of the new writers on the Times Fanzone is a self proclaimed "freelance sports journalist currently in my 3rd year at Cardiff University studying journalism" (i.e. a student) who really shows some passion for his articles. His latest one starts by discussing the Rams player turnover. According to his calculations "of their [that's our] 16-man squad the average time since each player signed is an incredibly low 8.8 months, that's 35 and a half weeks". There's a fact for you to quote before tomorrows match. Whoever said students had too much time on their hands?
(Before all student readers desert me en masse - I've been there).

March 30th

I was just thinking the other day what a great player Tito Villa is - shame on the Jackal for making snide remarks about him. Seriously though, it shows what a crazy season this is. Before this weekend, Villa had done very little to impress bar his goal at St Andrews (I had to give marks out of 10 for the Observer that day. I'd decided on 3 for Villa as he'd done nothing. I think I gave him 7 or 8 in the end). Now he's joint top scorer and let's face it, a couple of goals in April will probably win him Player of the Year (including my vote, in spirit at least). If only we'd have swapped our tickets for him (see March 27th), we could have sold him to Fiorentina for £5m and retired. On the subject of tickets, we had another massive crowd yesterday. I thought yesterday: you have to commend the marketing team, as I sat there in my free seat surrounded by everyone else who uses the same sports centre.

Record Breaking Rams

(written for the Times Fanzone)

Over the past few weeks, the media have increasingly speculated about which particular "worst ever" records Derby will break. Saturday saw an impressive hat-trick of: joint longest Premier League run without a win; first team to be relegated during March; the clubs longest winless streak.
The clubs new American owners General Sports Entertainment are quite big on "the match day experience" so I was disappointed not to see a hologram of Roy Castle appear at the final whistle, in the style of the absent Robbie Williams at a Take That concert. I can only think that the trumpet blast of "*Dedication's what you need*" put them off.

The game itself was billed "...THE WORST PREMIER FIXTURE EVER?" on Saturday morning (by a red top known in previous decades as The Daily Maxwell) due to the Rams well documented situation, coupled with Fulham's dire away record. The analysis after the game was not so harsh, proving that The Worst Premier Fixture Ever is most likely to be a mid-table stalemate in January rather than a match between two teams both going for victory.

Derby's goal bonanza also inched us further towards (or away from?) various low scoring records and a point is always cause for celebration. Interestingly, Tito Villa's two goals propelled him to the Rams joint top scorer in the league (he already had one) and with one of his rivals being a midfielder who left in January (Matt Oakley) he could well win an accolade of his own.

After the week he's had, Paul Jewell was probably quite relieved to have been playing Fulham. Judging by my trips to Craven Cottage, Fulham probably have the most genteel fans in the league and almost definitely the lowest numbers of NOTW readers per head. Therefore, there was no mass abuse from the visitors. If Derby had been hammered, the Rams fans might well have composed a few songs of our own. As it turned out it was an easy ride for the man known from his Bradford days as "Jagger".

So overall, not a bad day for the Rams despite our record breaking: a couple of goals, a point and most importantly a performance that if not brilliant, hinted that we don't need a complete new team. Carroll, Jones and Ghaly all showed quality whilst Villa and Sterjovski are doing their acclimatising now and should hit the ground running next season. Whether Ghaly will be here next season is anyone's guess. After his impressive cameo at 'Boro last week, Jewell said that if he kept it up we might sign him. In reality, if he keeps it up, the Championship won't be his best offer. It's just a shame that Stubbs is still absent as the past fortnight might have seen us yield 4 points rather than 1.

April 2008

Premier League Table 1st April 2008

		P	W	D	L	Pts	GD
17	Birmingham	32	7	9	16	30	-11
18	Bolton	32	6	8	18	26	-18
19	Fulham	32	4	12	16	24	-24
20	Derby	32	1	8	23	11	-51

Results:

06.04.08 Everton 1-0 Derby County

12.04.08 Derby County 0-6 Aston Villa

19.04.08 West Ham 2-1 Derby County

28.04.08 Derby County 2-6 Arsenal

The Rams came into April still needing four points to avoid the lowest ever Premier League tally but the month offered plenty of potential. Everton, Villa and West Ham had little to play for and were all experiencing indifferent form. Arsenal were out of the title race but safe in third and starting to blood young players.

I can't remember exactly why I had a shred of optimism left but it certainly wasn't justified. The Rams suffered four straight defeats and conceded six in each of the home fixtures. I'd be interested to know how many professional clubs have ever conceded six in consecutive home games before - yet another Premier League record I'm sure.

The away matches weren't nearly as bad and the Rams lost by a single goal on each occasion. Uncharacteristically, the Rams dominated large spells of both games but soft goals and missed chances meant another zero return.

With the season now completely written off, the Rams were starting to build for next campaign both on and off the pitch. Stan Ternent left to become the new Huddersfield manager and was replaced within a day by Jewell's ex-Wigan sidekick Chris Hutchings (Earlier in the season, Hutchings had a Sammy Lee style coach-to-manager-to-sack spell as Jewell's successor at Wigan). Jewell also made his first signing since relegation with the free transfer of Australian under-23 international Reuben Zadkovich.

Despite the complete debacle of the current season, Jewell was confident of a bright future, telling us: "I almost wish people could open the doors and see what is going on [at Moor Farm] as it is an exciting time" and "there are no guarantees… but what I am saying to supporters is that I think we will get promotion. I really do".

A footnote to the off-the-field planning was the announcement of a partnership arrangement with Dutch side FC Utrecht. Unlike other arrangements, this was two clubs of similar size and ambition rather than a "feeder club" arrangement. How this would work in practice remained to be seen.

As the season progressed, Rams fans were gaining more and more plaudits for the loyalty and humour shown, including the Nuts Magazine Supporters of The Year award - but more of that in the Journals. What continued to baffle many people is quite how the Rams continued to sell out almost every home game. Not just against the Big Four but even matches against Fulham and Sunderland were virtually sold out.

Speaking from my own perspective, it seemed the less we achieved, the more I wanted to be there for when we finally did score or even win. It still felt as though a win might just happen and after enduring all the torture thus far, I wanted a piece of anything good that might happen. Although it never came, I wasn't alone. Not only did home crowds sell-out but thousands of fans continued to travel away. Little did we know that the final "I was there" moment had already happened - seven months ago in September against Newcastle.

April 2nd

It's truly amazing that Barnsley have managed to beat Liverpool and Chelsea this season. Both fielded strong sides and the Liverpool victory was even at Anfield. Compare this to Barnsley's league form where they get turned over most weeks and are only outside the relegation zone on goal difference. The one notable difference between the league and cup teams is two players who are both cup tied but tend to be automatic choices in the league: Lewin Nyatanga and Jon Macken. Coincidence? Maybe, maybe not.

April 3rd

I was asked to write a 110 word preview of the Everton game for the Observer with another dozen on who is "due a big game". Here's what I sent:

On F.A. Cup weekend, it's worth noting that Oldham have won at Goodison Park this season and Barnsley have beaten both Liverpool and Chelsea. After over 30 league games, Derby still haven't managed to shock anyone with most results going to form. Given our form, that's not a good thing. Could this be our chance against an out of sorts and injury hit Everton? The Rams "officially" have nothing to lose now so will hopefully play without the fear that has paralysed us away from home on so many occasions. We still want points and goals and will be going for both.

Due a big game:

Robbie Savage - He could be in for a very busy afternoon given Everton's formation.

I wrote the piece shortly before going to bed last night and experienced a strangely lucid dream. We were playing Everton and I felt ashamed because I'd nominated Savage yet our midfield was: Lewis; Ghaly; Jones...and Malcolm! We won the game 1-0 thanks to an Eddie Lewis goal (he whacked in a rebound from a Kenny Miller shot - the dream was that detailed), as I walked home, I saw the Jackal surrounded by women in a Bingo Hall. What could it all mean? I'm trying to work out which bits of it were surrealist fantasy and which bits weren't. So far I've only discounted Bob Malcolm ever playing for the Rams again. I think it all means - have a bet on Derby to win 1-0 and Lewis to be first goal scorer...I'm off to check the odds.

April 4th

The odds on Eddie Lewis being first goal scorer and Derby winning 1-0 at Everton are 344/1. I've had a quid on that, £2 on Lewis to be first scorer at 40/1 and a quid on Earnie at 16/1. I've also had a pessimistic quid on the draw at 4/1 just in case the game doesn't go as I anticipate.

I mentioned my premonition at work a couple of times today. Funnily enough both people asked me if I caught the goal time. I used the same gag on both occasions "I'll go for a kip and let you know in half an hour" as I walked off smiling, they were no doubt shaking their head thinking "David Icke".
(See yesterdays if this sounds even more bonkers than it is already)

April 6th

When I'm fast asleep tonight, I expect to hear a booming voice in my mind saying "Sorry my child, I didn't realise Eddie Lewis was playing left back". You have to speculate to accumulate and for three quid, not only could I have won £400+ but could also have sold a couple of interviews to The Star or The Sport on the back of the divine intervention and then bagged a couple of reality TV slots. As it is, I'll have to keep my day job for a while. You may also be questioning the Earnshaw bet but as any seasoned gambler knows, I'll get my money back on that one as he wasn't on the pitch when the goal went in. 16/1 is always worth a punt for a centre forward, especially one who is overdue a goal to such an extent that medical experts are currently trying to induce one.

April 7th

An Article written for the Times Fanzone post Everton match. The title foresaw who would eventually get promoted. Unfortunately I didn't have a bet on it:

A Lesson for Stoke and Hull

A few of the teams Derby have signed players from since January: Blackburn, Rangers, Man City, Tottenham, Everton. A few of the teams that players have left The Rams first team to join: Plymouth, Leicester, Stoke, Ipswich, Barnsley. When Craig Fagan left his right wing slot to become Hull's fourth choice striker it said everything, although I'd started to get the hint when our captain and centre forward both made a smooth transition to a club 5 places from League 1.

With due respect to the Championship, there is an obvious point about quality here but I don't think that needs pointing out to anyone reading this. However, aside from quality, what Jewell has brought in is some experience of playing at the top level. In this parallel universe of Derby County where progress can only be charted by the manner and severity of defeat, the past month (with the exception of Chelsea away) hasn't been at all bad.

When we got promoted last May, it was clear Derby weren't world beaters but we had a clutch of players at a good age: Bywater, Mears, McEveley, Leacock, Jones, Barnes, Pearson, Nyatanga (some would even add Fagan) who all had the potential to establish themselves as Premier League players. Without discussing case by case, it's fair to say that the group has gone collectively backwards, some literally in the football pyramid. Players drained of confidence in a team drained of confidence with nowhere to look for guidance or leadership.

You only have to see the resurgent David Jones, now alongside Savage and Ghaly, to wonder how different the season could have been with a different approach to the transfer market. In a team with shattered confidence, no one wanted the ball from Jones and when they did, the hot potato was soon surrendered. Now, Jones can pass and move, play a one-two and has now started shooting with confidence. The contrast between Stubbs' presence (2 draws in 3) and Stubbs' absence (3 single goal defeats in 4 games and a draw with a pair of soft goals) is also telling.

Well, no point crying over spilt milk but if you happen to be the manager of Stoke, Bristol City or Hull, you may want to take note: don't do your shopping in the Championship. We have learnt the hard way, Sunderland have learnt the expensive way. Now the best the Rams can hope for a few more spirited performances and a revived Mears, McEveley and Leacock. If Jones' comeback is anything to go by, we could have half a team in no time.

April 9th

Derby's proposed link up with Dutch side FC Utrecht is an interesting story. An optimist might think "this really shows some ambition and provides some substance to the more abstract notion of international links. If it's alright for Man U then it's alright for us". It might also provide a tenuous reason for a Ramspace trip to the Low Countries. However, a more cynical person might be thinking "which player in particular from our bottom-of-the-league-with-no-wins-all-season reserve team would you like to borrow for your forthcoming fixtures against Ajax, PSV and Feyenoord? In fact, is there anyone you could lend *us*?"

My view is that if we're in a position when our reserves are good enough for the Dutch First Division then we're doing alright. Better than this season at any rate.

April 10th

The comment about Nyatanga and Macken last week got a mention on the SSA forum *[Sheep Shag Army]*. I'd like nothing more than to see Nyatanga succeed and be a home grown part of the Rams future but...
Playing for Wales has undoubtedly increased Nyatanga's stock over the years, especially when he was 17 and playing alongside a defence of Gabbidon, Delaney and Bale whilst rubbing shoulders with Giggs, Bellamy and Davies in the dressing room. I saw the team for the last Wales international though and his defensive cronies were from Oldham, Hull, Stockport and Peterborough. I couldn't help wondering how good you had to be?

Even so, he's been Wales regular for a couple of years and playing a full season in the Championship is good going for any 19 year old. I vote to bring him back on board...then lend him to FC Utrecht.

April 13th

(Written after the 0-6 Villa debacle)
Around half past two yesterday afternoon, we were sat in the pub surrounded by empty bottles of Fruuli and generally having a good time. I mentioned calling a taxi a couple of times but we had yet to do so. The Jackal then suggested that we forget about the game altogether with the reasoning "the tickets are paid for" (i.e. it wouldn't cost us any more *not* to go). Almost every matchday has run a similar course this season; great pre-

match banter and general chat, abruptly ended by going to the stadium. The afternoon generally goes downhill from there. I was the first to cave in though and Boab duly made the phone call for a taxi.

Stan Ternent's book he says that in times of adversity, he doesn't hide in the dug out but makes himself as visible as possible to take any flak from the crowd and deflect some from the players. Having recently read the book on a fast plane to China, the Jackal commented that he thought Stan would be out at 0-3. Within seconds Stan was stood, arms folded at the edge of the technical area. Our little chuckle was probably the highlight of the first half (me not being the type to clap the opposition for moments of quality).

At half time I recalled the Jackals earlier logic - it's not going to cost me anything to leave the stadium now. Considering the likely outcome of the second half, I reasoned that in the best case we might score a consolation and end up losing 1-3. In the worst case Villa might go on to win by four or five. I had little interest in either scenario. So after over two decades of watching the Rams, I left early. Not with ten minutes to go but at half time with hundreds more. It wasn't anger or protest, simply that our afternoon out would be better spent as it had been earlier, sat in the boozer and having a laugh - now with the added bonus of Sky Sports News. (An extended remix of this will appear on the Times Fanzone and the main site)

Full Times Fanzone article:
The Second Goal Was Offside!
Around half past two on Saturday afternoon, I was sat in the pub with a few friends having a good time. I had mentioned calling a taxi a couple of times but we'd put it off. One of the party then suggested that we forget about the game altogether. Almost every match-day has run a similar course this

season; great pre-match banter and general chat, abruptly ended by going to the stadium. The afternoon generally goes downhill from there. As my Dad likes to say "we had a great day apart from the ninety minutes in the middle". We caved in though and phoned a taxi to the ground.

On the way to Pride Park I was thinking about Queen of the South's win over Aberdeen earlier in the day: "If Queen of the South can beat Aberdeen and Aberdeen can draw with Bayern Munich, then given the opportunity, Queen of the South would obviously beat Bayern Munich. This being the case, surely a Rams victory over Villa isn't too much to ask?" The first 15-20 minutes seemed to be going fine with Derby having the majority of play. Then the problems started - Villa scored before they'd even had a proper shot as Carroll uncharacteristically misjudged a floated free kick and it went straight in. Within a minute it was 2-0 with Agbonlahor both offside and most definitely interfering (the ball hit him as Carroll was trying to get past him). Soon after Carroll's misery was compounded (but not completed) when a flat kick out which would usually result in a midfield scramble was returned over his head for 0-3. It would be a gross injustice to Stan Petrov to describe the goal as "lucky" as it was a perfectly executed outside-of-the-foot half-volley into the top corner from the half way line. However, to be on the receiving end of what was labelled in one paper as "goal of the season" was unlucky from a Rams perspective. It doesn't take much for Derby heads to drop and chins were collectively in chests of both players and fans at this point. Meanwhile, Villa fans were doing the conga.

At half time, I recalled my friends earlier logic for not going to the match and thought "it's not going to cost me anything to leave the stadium now". Considering the likely outcome of the second half, I reasoned that in the best case we might score a consolation and end up losing 1-3. In the worst case Villa might go on to win by four or five. I had little interest in either scenario. So after over two decades of watching the Rams, I left early.

Not with ten minutes to go but at half time with hundreds more. It wasn't anger or protest, simply that our afternoon out would be better spent as it had been earlier, sat in the boozer and having a laugh - now with the added bonus of Sky Sports News.

Another sorry episode in the season of Derby County. For fans of other clubs who can't ever imagine strolling out at half time, I would have agreed completely if it wasn't for the repeated new lows of this season. Never mind, I'd perked up by the time I got home.

April 15th

It looks like someone at the Daily Mirror has got their hands on a copy of Stan The Man (either that or they've been reading Ramspace). In a paragraph entitled "County taking Tern for worse" it begins by saying "The Premier League table suggests that Stan Ternent's stint as Derby assistant boss cannot be rated a complete success" before giving a couple of choice quotes from his book and suggesting Adam Pearson should have read it. (Can *anything* associated with Derby County this season be described as a complete success? In a list of people to blame for the debacle, Stan would probably sit about 37th, between the ex-DVD analyst and Benny Feilhaber). One of the quotes is about Stan's GBH on Jagger during their respective Burnley and Bradford days. Of course, this was brought to you in full weeks ago. For new readers, or those wishing to relive the moment, turn back to February 28th.

April 16th

Latest Fagan news...

Last month Fago left his Premier League berth on the right wing to join Hull on loan. "He wants to play up-front and there is an opportunity at Hull for him to do that" according to Jewell. Craig starts a couple of games up front and gets injured. When fit again, he finds himself on the bench behind Campbell, Windass and Folan. Last night, Craig returned to the first team and guess what? The man with a goal scoring record that makes Kenny Miller look like Dixie Dean is back on the right wing.

That reminds me, I must buy him a card. It's the first anniversary of his last league goal. (Leicester away last year, which I think was around this time).

April 17th

A woman at work, who has no interest or knowledge of football, told me yesterday how she had crossed the path of "a Derby County player" on an internet dating site. They'd looked at each others profiles but the romance ran aground when she asked something like "should I have heard of you?" It would be unfair of me to speculate on the identity of the player given her vague description. For all I know, it could have been an old picture of Tommy Johnson or Mark Pembridge.

April 21st

The way The Verdict works in The Observer is: someone from the paper gives you a ring after the match around half past six and you chat for ten minutes or so. The aspiring journalist then pieces together a paragraph about the match based on your conversation. I say aspiring as I presume someone working on a Saturday night to ring up the likes of us isn't quite ready for a Pulitzer prize. You never quite know which fragments of your conversation will be pounced upon.

On Saturday, by the time our man received the call, he had enjoyed a good day in the capital and had a few drinks along the way. Imagine his surprise on Sunday morning when the Observer results section contained a big picture of Alan Stubbs with the tag line "Player of the day: 'Stubbs had a blinding game - a West Ham friend reckons he's the fattest in the Premier League, but he held us together".

April 22nd

Simon's plea to get Pesch on the coaching staff a couple of days ago *(this refers to a video link not required in paper format!)* made me realise that in his brief and often forgotten spell assisting Terry Westley, Pesch was one of our better no. 2s in recent years. Compared to Ned Kelly, Holdsworth and any post-McClaren Smith assistant (Trewick, Crosby), there's not much competition. (I'll reserve judgement on Stan).

With new Academy Director Phil Cannon on the back page of tonight's Telegraph, it's worth looking at a game during the Westley era. When we drew against Hull at home we had five home grown players on duty: Camp, Holmes, Barnes, Nyatanga, and Addison making his debut. According to my calculations, Miles Addison was the last home-grown Rams league debutant - almost two years and two weeks to the day.

April 23rd

Following yesterdays piece, I had a quick look at The Complete Record and saw that we used 10 home grown players during the 2005/6 season. In addition to those mentioned, Pablo Mills, Marcus Tudgay, Lee Grant, Nathan Doyle and Lionel Ainsworth also appeared. Add to that Jacko, Bolder and Boets who were all signed as kids for nominal fees and you have thirteen players for the price of Gary Teale. Considering some of the rubbish and mediocrity that has been through the revolving doors in the last couple of years (and under Phil Brown) it begs a few questions such as: has our young talent dried up in the last couple of years?; Have our scouting networks done anything?; How much cash would we have saved if we'd have just shouted down the corridor instead of signing Thome, Thirwell, Fadiga, Currie, Macken, Ryan Smith...the list goes on.

April 24th

The big news today was Journals hero Stan Ternent leaving us to take over at Huddersfield. I had to smile at Adam Pearson graciously saying "We have not sought compensation from Huddersfield". I wonder what the going rate is for a 62 year old assistant implicated in one of the biggest footballing debacles ever known? Jewell was obviously gutted "We already have a new assistant lined up and ready to start work tomorrow". I bet Jagger had Stan's cones and bibs boxed up before you could say "Chris Hutchings in reception for you Paul".

Good luck to Stan though, I hope to see him back at Pride Park one day, facing up the crowd on the edge of the away technical area.

April 26th

A preview of the Arsenal game written for The Observer:
With only three games remaining this season, it looks increasingly likely that Derby will go down in history as, statistically, the worst Premier League team ever. To use the old cliché - the League table doesn't lie and with one win all season, it's very difficult to present an argument to the contrary. A good argument would be to say "well, we did beat Arsenal". Arsenal's season seems to have run aground so some end of season silliness is always a possibility. We haven't fared badly against the Big Four at home this season, so hopefully it will be a good night on the Rams Farewell Tour.
Due a Big Game:
Kenny Miller - Supposedly our top striker but hasn't scored this year in the league.

April 27th

Ramspace have had the following request:

"You may not be aware of this but Derby County have won something this year - the Nuts Football Awards for the best fans of the season.

We are producing the television show of the awards for MTV and we're planning to come up to Pride Park for the home game against Arsenal to interview some fans. We'll also be bringing a couple of the Nuts girls along to present the award and provide a good photo opportunity so we need some diehard derby fans to take part and I thought you might be the best place to start."

Chris gave them a ring and this was the outcome:

"Lads,

I have spoken to the producer and the format of this is basically they are going to get some form of trailer delivered to PP around 3pm. Basically he wants the two girls to be in the truck and they will give (the depressed) Derby fans a cup of tea, a biscuit and talk about the season.

The interviews will be 1 by 1 and I guess they'll edit the best bits together. He is very keen to get a shot of lads queuing up for the trailer. Ideally he wants 8 or 10 but doesn't want to send the girls out to get lads unless they have to. They also want someone to present the trophy to. He said he was looking to do the interviews between 18.00 and 18.30. I am apparently going to get a contact phone number before Monday.

If you want to google the two girls, I am reasonably sure the names he mentioned were Kayleigh Pearson and Lindsay Strutt."

A few of us can make this but we could do with a few more volunteers. If anyone is going to the match, can be there for 18:00-18:30 and fancies it, drop me an email on s_spaceram@post.com before about 2pm. I'll find out more tomorrow about where they will be etc. and let you know.

In the unlikely event that I'm inundated, you're welcome to come for the "queuing shots" later on!

April 29th

Never let it be said that Ramspace are snobbish because we do a turn for The Observer and The Times on occasions. Yesterday, we gathered together a few lads for Nuts magazine. The gist of what Nuts wanted to do is covered by the previous entry - in practice it was somewhere between Carry on Camping and Blur's Country House video. The theme of "tea and sympathy" was that the girls gave the lads a cup of tea then asked about the season. On receiving his cup of tea, one of us quipped "that's the only cup we'll be getting this season" to much laughter. It was a brief insight into the process to see that this needed three takes - by which time we could have also done with some canned laughter.

After the interviews we had to display some acting worthy of a BAFTA. One of us left the van (on the count of three) to be waved off by the girls. The same girl then called "who's next?" to the chap waiting outside the van. Queuing up for "tea and sympathy" was the theme but innuendo was thinly veiled. One of the girls' sound check of "who's next for sloppy's?" said it all.

All in all, a good laugh and strange insight into the media world. From what I can gather, the models are highly regarded in their field yet were basically a couple of girls doing a days work. We were surprised when one of them told us she'd had driven up in a far from glamorous car - "lifestyles of the rich and shameless eh?", luckily she either didn't hear the comment or didn't get it.

April 30th

Last week I wrote a bit about the absence of young players this season and the Player of the Year awards really brought this home. The winner of Young Player of the Year was Lewis Price, who at 23 must have been pushing the upper age limit. The award also said a lot about Dean Leacock's season. For some people, Leacock was a contender for the Player of the Year proper last season and he was expected to take the Premier League in his stride. Now he's demoted to the "Young" shortlist and losing out to a player who was signed as back up and played only because of injuries.

May 2008

Premier League Table 1st May 2008

		P	W	D	L	Pts	GD
17	Reading	36	9	6	21	33	-28
18	Birmingham	36	7	11	18	32	-17
19	Fulham	36	6	12	18	30	-25
20	Derby	36	1	8	27	11	-63

Results:

03.05.08 Blackburn 3-1 Derby County

11.05.08 Derby County 0-4 Reading

Going into May, it was still possible for the Rams to reach 15 points. Blackburn away was a potential point given our last two away performances and Reading at home had been viewed for months as an opportunity to get all three. The inevitable happened and the Rams lost twice - conceding an early lead at Blackburn to lose 1-3 followed by one of the worst matches of the season. Reading had gone into free fall during the final stages of the season and were now facing relegation - there would be no end of season party. Reading *had* to beat the Rams to have any chance of staying in the Premier League.

Reading duly rolled the Rams over 0-4 in one of the most spineless Rams performances witnessed by anyone in the sell-out crowd. Up until now, Rams fans had shown unbelievable restraint in the face of one disaster after another. Finally, the fans turned as a chorus of "you're not fit to wear the shirt" filled the stadium and many players were booed. Reading won easily but were still relegated - an unhappy afternoon all round. Rams fans invaded the pitch at the final whistle, ruling out the traditional "lap of honour" for the last home game of the season. It was probably best all round.

The Journals of Derventio – May

May 1st

The Nuts episode is seemingly not over with a potential Ramspace invite to the WKD Nuts Football awards in London next week. Watch this space. All I can say is that whoever did the acting on Monday must have put in a truly storming performance. When I found out the Rams had won Supporters of the Year, I let the Derby Telegraph know. I thought: an award from a national publication; a good news story; a Derby County story; and a good news Derby County story - a rarity this season. Also apt because the Telegraph has been running daily Supporter of the Year profiles along the lines of "Ethel from Allenton has had a season ticket since the 60's". I didn't even get the courtesy of a reply. Meanwhile, Monday's paper ran a big picture story of a woman who found a bird nest in her house and also reported the theft of a rabbit and cage.

May 4th

Now it's official that we're going to get the lowest ever Premier League points tally, it occurred to me how many times we've revised (i.e. lowered) our targets this season. First off, it was the usual 42 for survival ("41 to go" after the Pompey game), then it became apparent that mid to upper 30s would be enough. Soon it was a case of just getting 15, which didn't seem too tall an order at the time. It's been like a Duckworth/ Lewis method to account for severe ongoing crapness rather than adverse weather. The latest one in my mind was - let's just win two games. For months Reading was nailed on for a dead end of season game where this could happen. Now what happens? After yesterdays sequence of results, Reading suddenly *have* to beat us. New target - concede less than a hundred goals this season. If we concede less than 15 it's party time!

May 5th

The season just goes from bad to worse for Robert Earnshaw. First he was continually left on the bench by both Davies and Jewell; secondly he was axed from the Wales squad for the first time in years; and now the final indignity - he failed to make a shortlist for the Premier League's best somersaults. The article in the Observer sports mag had a British Olympic gymnast rating six players includng Lua Lua who hasn't played in the Premier League since last season and Wigan's Aghahowa who I can't ever remember scoring, although a photo of him mid air in a Wigan kit suggests he has. Earnie's effort against Arsenal was evidently too late.

For the record, Aghahowa got a perfect "10" for his "half twist into quintuple back flip". The gymnast was less complimentary towards Nani of whom he said "It just looks like he chucks himself. I'm not surprised Alex Ferguson told him to cut it out" accompanied by a picture of Nani in a pose that wouldn't look out of place alongside a twin tower.

May 6th

I hope our summer spending isn't too reliant on the Fagan deal becoming permanent. The Hull Fan At Work printed off a few responses to a Fagan story on a Hull website. The comments included: "..he has done nothing since he came back"; "...send him back at the end of the season" and a particularly harsh one "...Fagan is useless and a liability. If he plays we don't stand a chance of going up...He was crap first time round. Gotta hand it to him tho' for taking the money and doing the square root of fcuk [sic] all".

May 8th

Last night was the Nuts Football Awards in London. There were six Rams fans there as far as I could see with our table being made up by a "celebrity" hairdresser and his mate there to present the "Dodgiest Barnet" award. It wasn't exactly a galaxy of stars but in attendance were: Steve Claridge, Dave Beasant, Warren Barton, Chris Kamara, Mark Bright, stacks of models and what appeared to be a couple of tables of young London footballers. (Text this morning - "Asked Kammy about Stan story last night. He said it's exactly how it happened" i.e. Stan Ternent roughing up Jagger at Bradford a few years ago). Everyone was generally quite friendly and Dave Beasant didn't even take offence when asked twice in five minutes about a girl he'd been seeing in Long Eaton.

The nicest bloke by far was Kevin Day who works on Match of The Day 2. Simon had met him before when being filmed by MOTD2 at the Fulham game and the acquaintance was soon renewed. Day was presenting the Bargain of the Year Award (nominees: Phil Jageilka, Ken Jones, Elano and winner Roque Santa Cruz) and made the best comment of the night by saying how strange it was to be reading a list of £5m-£6m players as "bargains" when clubs were going out of business for the sake of a hundred grand. Completely out of kilter with the frivolous style of the ceremony and the host was dumbstruck - his autocue hadn't seen that one coming. The host, by the way, was MTV/ T4 host Dave Berry.

When our big moment came, Simon had been nominated by the producer to collect the award from an ex-Big Brother contestant, Chanelle. Dave Berry opened with something about Chanelle wanting to be a WAG, Chanelle pointed to a table of skeleton thin models drinking WKD from Champagne glasses and replied "I think it's that table". Ever the professional, Berry moved swiftly to Simon and asked something along the lines of "you're the worst team in Premier League history...etc...now you're getting an award from Chanelle" to which Simon responded with a quip like "it gets worse, an award from another loser" (the exact transcript of this exchange is in the brain cells destroyed by complimentary ice buckets of

Champers, WKD and beer with cocktails on the side). We were soon off the stage. I'd love to see how this section of the night is edited.

It was then backstage for photos of us, the trophy and Chanelle, with Simon assuring her he was only joking. By the time we returned to the main hall, the ceremony was coming to a close...and then the aftershow. Another hour or so and I had to head back to the train station, the night rounded off by a shout of "Up the Rams" from someone as I charged down the escalator in Rams shirt and blazer.

An article on the Nuts episode written on request for the Times on-line. As you'll see, there is quite a bit borrowed directly from the Journals but it earned us a magnum of Champagne as "poster of the month".

The Rams goes Nuts!

You may be aware from our previous entry that unlike Arsenal and Liverpool, The Rams did not end the season empty handed after scooping the Nuts Football Awards Supporters of the Season. The first we heard was from an email to the Ramspace Editor, Nuts were coming to Pride Park with some "Nuts girls", could we find some willing volunteers for a bit of filming? The premise as summarized by the editor was "basically he wants the two girls to be in the truck and they will give (the depressed) Derby fans a cup of tea, a biscuit and talk about the season." Needless to say, we managed to find a couple of volunteers...

Never let it be said that Ramspace are snobbish because we do bits for The Observer and Times Online. The gist of what Nuts wanted to do is stated in the intro but using a camper van rather than the elaborate media truck we anticipated. In practice it was somewhere between Carry on Camping and Blur's Country House video.

The theme of "tea and sympathy" was that the girls gave us a cup of tea then asked about the season. On receiving his cup of tea, a mate quipped "that's the only cup we'll be getting this season" to much laughter. It was a brief insight into the process to see that this needed three takes - by which time we could have also done with some canned laughter.

Next it was on to the Awards ceremony at Cafe de Paris off Leicester Square. It wasn't exactly a galaxy of stars but in attendance were: Steve Claridge, Dave Beasant, Warren Barton, Chris Kamara, Mark Bright, stacks of models and what appeared to be a couple of tables of young London footballers.

The nicest bloke by far was Kevin Day who works on Match of The Day 2. He chatted to us for quite a while and had previously met one of our lads when MOTD2 filmed the Rams at Fulham.

Day was presenting the Bargain of the Year Award (nominees: Phil Jageilka, Ken Jones, Elano and winner Roque Santa Cruz) and made comment of the night by saying how strange it was to be reading a list of £5m-£6m players as "bargains" when clubs were going out of business for the sake of a hundred grand. It was a timely reminder that life exists outside the Premier League and completely out of kilter with the frivolous style of the ceremony.

When our moment came, we were called to collect the award from an ex-Big Brother contestant, Chanelle.

The host Dave Berry pointed the microphone to our man and asked something along the lines of "you're the worst team in Premier League history...etc...now your getting an award from Chanelle" to which we responded with a quip like "it gets worse, an award from another loser" (the exact transcript of this exchange is in the brain cells destroyed by complimentary ice buckets of Champers, WKD and beer with cocktails on the side). We were soon off the stage with our contribution edited out for the silver screen.

It was then onto the aftershow and a chat with a few of the ex-footballers present, all of who it has to be said were up for a chat and some banter.

One of the briefest chats of the evening was with ex- Rams full-back Warren Barton. After an opening gambit of "things have been going downhill ever since we signed you" I suppose it's not surprising. At least we didn't ask him for a lift home in his limo.*

Once we had scooped the award, the girls were queuing up to be see with us...ok, every five minutes one the lads would shout "quick, it's Naomi, 23 from Doncaster, grab the camera"

Barton, along with fellow ex-Rob Lee, had recently been arrested on suspicion of the bizarre charge of joyriding in a limousine.

May 11th

(pre-Reading game)

An end of season review written for the Observer in 210 words or less (the printed version was edited down even more):

How was your season?

As Birmingham were recruiting from Arsenal and Juventus and Sunderland were spending £6-£9m per player, we were signing a 33 year old from League 1. It wasn't just about the money; the Premier League was far better than Billy Davies anticipated.

We weren't exactly expecting Europe but I don't think any Rams fan expected what was to come. We were at times outclassed but the most frustrating thing was to see us continually lose the closer games by inexplicable errors.

Happy with the gaffer?

He hasn't won a game and his signings haven't delivered yet. However, so far he has emerged blameless. There's a huge expectation for next season and Jewell is making all the right noises. Ask me again at Christmas.

Who were the stars – and who flopped?

Darren Moore was expected to play a dozen games at most but has been there all season so credit to him but it doesn't say much for Davis, Todd and Leacock. The strikers have collectively failed and half the squad were back in the Championship by March.

Who were the best and worst away fans?

Best - Man Utd. backed their team to the hilt in a tight game.

Worst - Arsenal sat in sulky silence when we equalised.

Top hate figure at another club?

We need to get our own house in order first.

Top five best opposition players?

Martin Petrov, Anelka (then Bolton), Torres, Adebayor, Gerrard

Who do you want to win the Champions League?

United

Fabio Capello? Not bothered

Game 39? Bad idea..

May 12th

Yesterdays game barely needs any comment. The greatest moment, possibly of the season, was at half time when I thought I'd lost £20. Returning to my seat quarter of an hour later, it was still lying untouched on the floor.

The Nuts awards were on TMF last night although our bit was quite brief with Simon's line to Chanelle completely edited out. My three year old niece said to me today "I saw you on telly last night". My Dad chipped in "I think she means some photos of you on the laptop". I said "Maybe...but I *was on telly last night*". It's not everyday you can say that.

Article written post Reading match

In Search of a Beer, 3 Points and Twenty Quid

The day had started badly. A fortnight ago Derby County had announced that, to commemorate a record breakingly bad season, today would be "Rams Day". A day all about the fans including a beer tent outside the ground. It was my idea to meet outside the ground and after two laps, I realised there was no beer tent. We all blamed the new American owners' grasp of the British licensing laws. A beer tent on a hot May day outside a football ground? The idea was far too good to be legal.

Twenty minutes later we were stood in a near deserted concrete tunnel, officially known as "the concourse" sipping over-priced and under-carbonated beer. We were inside the ground already and one step closer to what was fully expected to be the worst part of the day...the match.

Derby County had had, officially, the worst Premier League season ever and this was the final game of the campaign. Weeks ago we had thought that Reading at home might yield some points but due to recent results, Reading now had to beat us to stay in the division. What was supposed to be an end of season kickabout was now another potential hammering.

The highlight of the first half was when a ball boy seated in front of us slipped en route to retrieve the ball. After being on the receiving end of several mocking chants, he responded with a rousing solo version of "Derby 'til I die, I'm Derby 'til I die..." and was joined on backing vocals by at least 5,000 fans.

167

We regrouped at half time and as I strode to the kiosk to buy another distraction from the football, I realised I had dropped a £20 note somewhere amongst the feet of the amassed 33,000. The 10 minutes chat at half time is one of the peaks of my social life at the moment but I was too depressed to make small talk - the match ticket was a waste of money, the drinks a further squeeze and now I've just thrown away what could have been lunch in town.

I trooped back to my seat with my chin firmly down - dejected but also looking for my twenty quid. And then, miracles do happen. On this breezy May afternoon, my neatly folded twenty pound note was waiting patiently below my seat. I couldn't disguise my delight and commented to the young lad in the next seat that he'd "slipped up there". Realising that it would have at least doubled his pocket money, I didn't labour the point. His face told me that he didn't share my joy.

As the final whistle blew, Rams fans poured onto the pitch after reminding the Police "two dogs, you've only got two dogs". I strolled across the hallowed turf minutes later. It provided me with a short cut to get out and finally draw a line under this awful season. By the way, the Rams had lost 4-0.

.

May 14th

Yet another embarrassment for the Rams - around Christmas time I compared the plight of Derby to Gretna in the Scottish Premier: both newly promoted; both getting hammered every week; both bottom of the league. At the time both clubs were hovering around the six point mark. Gretna gradually began to pull away until financial disaster struck. Firstly players were sold and then the administrators stepped in. This lead to a ten point deduction and half the depleted squad being made redundant including anyone likely to find another club (i.e. players who were any good). Last night Gretna beat Hearts 1-0 to reach 13 points. Despite the clubs mid season implosion, they *still* managed to surpass the Rams points total with a 10-point handicap.

*

Final Premier League Table 2008

		P	W	D	L	Pts	GD
17	Fulham	38	8	12	18	36	-22
18	Reading	38	10	6	22	36	-25
19	Birmingham	38	8	11	19	35	-16
20	Derby	38	1	8	29	11	-69

Epilogue

When the transfer window closed on September 1ˢᵗ 2008, Paul Jewell had signed a total of 14 new players to add to his captures of the previous January. The Rams had lost three of their first four fixtures and were bottom of the Championship. And then…

…on Saturday September 13ᵗʰ, Derby County beat Sheffield United 2-1 at Pride Park to record Paul Jewell's first victory as Derby County manager. The win came 361 days after the victory over Newcastle, narrowly avoiding a full calendar year without a league victory.

APPENDIX

What are The Journals of Derventio?

Ramspace evolved from The Baseball Bat Fanzine, a bi-monthly Derby County on-line fanzine. When we changed from BBF to Ramspace, we wanted to make the zine a live site to capture things as they happened. In the old format, articles could date quickly or ideas could be irrelevant by the time an issue was due.

In keeping with this, the Journals is an opportunity to comment on things as they happen; share stories, facts and stats; use ideas that don't justify a full article; and write about anything else of interest. It's not the intention for The Journals to be a soapbox so it would be more accurately seen as "Ramspace Daily" than a self-obsessed blog.

The main focus is of course our beloved Rams but The Journals will happily stray off-piste at times to capture anything you'd discuss over a virtual pint. Ramspace has readers outside Derby and outside the UK so I try to give our absent friends a taste of the day-to-day struggles and humour of supporting The Rams where possible; a perspective you might miss on the official sites.

Who's Who?

When reading The Journals, you will see various characters referred to from time to time. Here's a brief introduction to some of them:

The Jackal

So called partly because of his elusive nature and partly a pun on his name. The majority of games I go to are with The Jackal so he tends to be on the scene a lot with a few wry comments and the occasional bit of exuberant behaviour e.g. losing his glasses on the pitch at Southampton away in the promotion season.

Simon

Ilkeston's greatest unknown football pundit. Simon's memory for football trivia is astonishing, especially considering the amount of grey matter destroyed during 15 years of a weekly pub-match-pub-club routine. Goalkeeping trivia is a speciality, for example the preferred kicking foot of any given Championship 'keeper.

A Hull Fan At Work

Self explanatory. A Hull fan exiled in Ilkeston who is generally one step ahead when it comes to anything Hull City related including Adam Pearson, Craig Fagan and Phil Brown.

Bob

Also referred to as Boab or Rockin' Bob, Bob has a season ticket next to the Editor. He is usually on the scene for any pre-match and post-match activities.

Chris (the editor)

Founded the Baseball Bat on-line Fanzine in May 2000 and has held a Season Ticket since the 1982/83 season. Chris maintains the overall running of Ramspace.

Me

A secondary partner in Ramspace, I had a season ticket from the age of about eight until a succession of living out the area, out the country, working weekends and being skint meant a spell without. I've now finally bought one again but it's a far cry from the early-mid nineties every game years.